Crisis Management
in the Age of Social Media

Crisis Management in the Age of Social Media

Louis Capozzi and Susan R. Rucci

First published in 2013 by
Business Expert Press, LLC
222 East 46th Street, New York, NY 10017
www.businessexpertpress.com

ISBN-13: 978-1-60649-580-3 (paperback)
ISBN-13: 978-1-60649-581-0 (e-book)

Business Expert Press Public Relations collection

Collection ISSN: 2157-345X (print)
Collection ISSN: 2157-3476 (electronic)

Cover and interior design by Exeter Premedia Services Private Ltd., Chennai, India

First edition: 2013

10 9 8 7 6 5 4 3 2 1

Printed in the United States of America.

Abstract

Social media has fundamentally changed the contract between institutions and their publics. Today, people expect a conversation, not a one-way diatribe. That, combined with the speed of the Internet, changes the game for anticipating, managing and ultimately avoiding a crisis. This book explores the challenges of managing crises in the age of social media.

Keywords

crisis management, crisis communication, crisis response, crisis prevention, social media crisis, social media, social media strategy, stakeholders Facebook, Twitter, tweet, Linkedin, Instagram, Tumblr, YouTube, public relations, corporate communication, reputation management, risk, natural disasters, accidents, customer complaints, rumors, rumor management, apologies.

Contents

Introduction ix

Chapter 1   The Age of The Instant Crisis 1

Chapter 2   Susan G. Komen's "Race for the Headlines"..................17

Chapter 3   #DearNetflix: I Am Cancelling My Subscription!
            Signed Social Media...25

Chapter 4   To Tweet or Not to Tweet? 37

Chapter 5   Bank of America Stands Down................................47

Chapter 6   The Friendly Skies Turn Ugly 55

Chapter 7   Racing from the Storm 77

Chapter 8   A Less Than "Progressive" Approach 87

Chapter 9   "Refrigerator Gate" in China 97

Chapter 10 Herding Cats—The Challenge of
            Controlling Employees......................................107

Chapter 11 Crisis Planning in the Conversation Age 117

Notes 125
References 133
Index 141

Introduction

I spent over 40 years in the public relations business, both as the leader of a major agency and the chief communications officer of a large insurance company. I witnessed and managed dozens of crisis situations over that career. And, I've seen "the golden hour" of crisis management turn into "golden minutes."

Now I teach a course on crisis management at New York University. My students selected a current crisis to review and wrote case studies analyzing the situations, evaluating the quality of the response based on the principles we had discussed in class. Each is given credit for their contributions later in this introduction.

Here's the assignment the students were given:

Analyze a crisis recently in the news. You may choose the corporation or organization that will be the subject of your research (no individuals), as well as the particular crisis experienced by that organization.

Using secondary research tools, describe the following:

- The nature of the crisis.
- When it was discovered.
- The timeliness of the organization's response to the crisis.
- The nature of the response.
- Any unintended consequences of the response.
- The effectiveness of the response.
- How individual constituencies were affected by the crisis and response.
- How the crisis was resolved, if it has been.
- Your assessment of what worked, what didn't and how the organization might have been more effective in its response.

Social media drove each and every one of the cases chosen by the students. That's not a coincidence. That's the new reality of crisis communication today. Now every crisis finds its way onto social media, either by accident or purpose, but always with consequences.

Until recently, I included a section in the course devoted to the role of social media in crisis management. But after this experience, I realized that social media had transformed the way every crisis emerges, how it's driven, and how it's handled. No longer could I teach a course on crisis management with a "section" on social media. The topic needed to be integrated into every facet of the course.

This book presents examples of social media-driven crises. We offer analyses of what went right, what went wrong, and how to learn from them for the future. The authors intend to offer readers a tool to learn from. If you work for an organization or a brand, the principles and cases discussed here should help you prepare for the time when—not "if"—you come under the hot lights of social media scrutiny.

Thanks to the students who contributed their case studies, which were edited and expanded by the authors. They include:

Pristina Alford

Bindya Bajaj

Erin Clark

Robin Drew

Kaycie East

Malorie Ginsberg

LoriBeth Greenan

Myriam Greene

Weisi (Tanja) Li

Ignacio Baleztena Navarrete

Susan Rucci

Kirsten Simmons

Bernice Stevens

One of those students, Susan Rucci, was not your typical graduate student. An Emmy award-winning producer, Susan has worked for CBS News, Retirement Living TV, Good Morning America, and CNBC. She covered some of the most groundbreaking news events of recent history including the O.J. Simpson trials (criminal and civil), Columbine School shootings, and D.C. Beltway Sniper attacks.

Susan traveled with and reported on the George W. Bush presidential campaign as a producer at CBS News. While at the network, she also witnessed the network undergo its own crisis, an early incarnation of social media. Bloggers questioned the authenticity of documents used in a "60 Minutes" report on President George W. Bush's experience in the Texas National Guard. The "Memogate" fallout resulted in numerous producers being fired and Dan Rather eventually stepping down as anchor of the "CBS Evening News." Susan observed how a crisis fueled by the online blogging community undermined a news organization that once had stellar reporting credentials. Now she's decided, mid-career, to change her focus to public relations. Her first-hand experience with crisis management as a journalist, along with her outstanding analytical and writing skills, made her a natural partner for me on this project.

Another student, Bernice Stevens, chose Crisis Management and Social Media as her capstone subject. Her thesis paper greatly informed the first and last chapters of this book.

Thanks also to Joe Gleason, former president of MSL North America. Joe and I worked side-by-side on a number of high-profile crises. Our clients included the American Medical Association, Denny's Restaurants, Mitsubishi Motors, and many others. Joe's presentation on what he called "The Crisis Crucible" provided great material for Chapter 1.

Finally, special thanks go to Dr. Helio Fred Garcia, a fellow professor at NYU, who designed the crisis management course and who provided much of the academic background for this book. Fred's material was particularly important for Chapter 1, which sets out some definitions and principles.

Louis Capozzi
New York University
New York, NY

CHAPTER 1

The Age of The Instant Crisis
(with Bernice Stevens)

Crises have existed as long as civilization itself. Caesar was murdered on the steps of the Theatre of Pompey in 44 BC. Henry VIII defied the Roman Catholic Church in 1534. The Great Chicago Fire killed hundreds in 1871. Nearly 150 garment workers were killed in 1904 in the Triangle Shirtwaist Factory because doors to stairwells and exits were locked. In more modern history world, leaders have been attacked and killed, and countries have faced the agony of attacks and wars.

What those challenges had in common was time—time to assess the situation, time to react, and time to repair.

But now the age of the *instant* crisis has arrived. Companies, non-profit organizations (NGOs), governments, and high-profile individuals often seem unable to cope. The ingredients include speed, pervasiveness, and huge numbers. Verizon adds a $2 charge, and one-hour later 100,000 signatures appear on a Twitter petition.

Type "social media crisis" into Google, you will get more than 44 million results. In the time it took to write this chapter, Progressive Insurance, Time Magazine and Fareed Zakaria, and MSNBC's Mark Halperin all suffered reputation damage fueled by social media.

Erik Qualman vividly portrays the change in the way people connect in the YouTube video http://www.youtube.com/watch?v=0eUeL3n7fDs based on his book—*Socialnomics: How Social Media Transforms the Way We Live and Do Business*.[1] Some of his most compelling factoids include:

- YouTube has become the second-largest search engine in the world.
- Social media has overtaken porn as the #1 activity on the Internet.
- One in eight couples married in the United States met online.
- If Facebook were a country, it would be the world's third largest.
- A New Linkedin member joins every second.
- Every minute, 24 hours of video is uploaded onto YouTube.
- If Wikipedia were a book, it would be 2.25 million pages long and take 23 years to read.
- Seventy-eight percent of consumers trust peer reviews. Only 14% trust advertisements.
- E-readers have surpassed traditional book sales.
- Kindergarteners learn on iPads now, not chalkboards.

So there is a new playing field—social media—and new rules of the game: analysis, action, and communication, all at high speed. Yet the realities of people's reasonable expectations and the basic rules guiding crisis behavior and communication have not changed.

The Social Media Landscape

Social media allows individuals to interact with one another, exchanging details about their lives, such as biographical data, professional information, personal photos, and up-to-the-minute thoughts using Internet-based software and interfaces (Investopedia).[2]

Driven by advancements in computer and mobile technologies, the social media landscape evolved radically in the last decade, influencing spheres of communication, business, and the practice of public relations. With the birth and failures of the first social networking sites, such as Geocities and SixDegrees.com, during the dot-com era, the use of online communities has since evolved far beyond the scope of anyone's imagination in the early days of dial-up Internet.

According to data released by comScore in the top 10 need-to-know about social networking and where it is headed study, social networking reached 82% of the world's online population by 2012, representing 1.2 billion users around the world (comScore.com).[3] The study found that social networking ranked as the most popular content category in worldwide engagement, accounting for 19% of all time spent online. It also found that nearly 1 in every 5 min spent online is now spent on social networking sites.

Data from the Pew Research Center demonstrate the pervasiveness of social media (see Table 1.1). Regardless of the age group, ethnicity, gender, or income level, the majority of the US population uses social media.[4]

Consequently, it has become increasingly critical for organizations of every kind to create an online presence extending beyond websites into social media. In doing so, they can reap the benefits of direct access to stakeholders. In *The New Rules of Marketing & PR*, David Meerman Scott explains, "The Internet is like a massive focus group with uninhibited customers offering up their thoughts for free!"[5] He affirms the "new rules" call for organizations and businesses to tap into the

Table 1.1. Who Uses Social Networking Sites
(% of internet users within each group who use social networking sites)

All internet users (n = 1,873)	69%
Men (n = 886)	63
Women (n = 987)	75*
Age	
18–29 (n = 351)	92***
30–49 (n = 524)	73**
50–64 (n = 567)	57*
65+ (n = 404)	38
Race/ethnicity	
White, Non-Hispanic (n = 1,355)	68
Black, Non-Hispanic (n = 217)	68
Hispanic (n = 188)	72
Annual household income	
Less than $30,000/yr (n = 469)	73*
$30,000–$49,999 (n = 356)	66
$50,000–$74,999 (n = 285)	66
$75,000+ (n = 501)	74**
Education level	
No high school diploma (n = 129)	65
High school grad (n = 535)	65
Some College (n = 513)	73*
College + (n = 692)	72*

Source: Pew Internet Civic Engagement Tracking Survey, July 16–August 07, 2012. N = 2,253 adults ages 18+. Interviews were conducted in English and Spanish and on landline and cell phones. Margin of error is ±3 percentage points.
*Statistically significant difference compared with others in the same grouping.

conversations happening in social networks to know what is being said. The value of knowing can help organizations develop communication and business strategies to address the needs of its stakeholders.

Social Media and Public Relations

As the social media landscape has evolved, public figures and organizations have adapted and built online communities to reach their stakeholders. The 2008 and 2012 presidential campaigns of Barack Obama provide evidence of the potential successes that may be gained through social media initiatives. His election and re-election were the result of an ingenious multi-media public relations campaign through which constituents were engaged via traditional advertising and various forms of social media, such as blogs and social networking sites. Facebook and Twitter, the most popular sites usually reserved for Gen Y communication, gave way to the greater purpose of disseminating useful information to citizens of all ages and, in turn, drove support for President Obama's campaigns. The President was also able to engage in authentic conversations with stakeholders. When he personally tweeted, he signed them with a "-bo." Those "autographed" tweets would be re-tweeted thousands of times, further capitalizing on social media's strengths.

For public relations professionals, the social media campaign, particularly in the 2008 campaign, redefined the practice of public relations as it demonstrated the potential for organizations to thrive in the social media space—an area that was largely unchartered territory prior to the election.

Since the election, social networking sites have become saturated with the likes of company-sponsored accounts, fan pages, and so forth. Furthermore, almost every political and corporate communication plan now includes a social media component. Although organizations understand there is a need to establish a presence via social media platforms, many struggle to find an effective means to communicate, solicit, and utilize feedback from stakeholders. To their dismay, many have mishandled and underestimated the power of the stakeholders' voice in the online space.

In *Reputation Management,* John Doorley and Helio Fred Garcia outline the broad characteristics of social media.[6] They emphasize authenticity, transparency, decentralization of authority, speed, and collaboration as primary characteristics. With the proper approach, these characteristics, as proven in the Obama campaigns, can be beneficial conduits for immediate reach and accessibility to stakeholders. However, in a crisis, they can be an asset *or* a liability. "Speed is a defining element of social media and a characteristic that presents challenges for organizations in reputation management. The pace at which information is shared and propagated in social media is faster and broader than older forms of communication."[7]

The *Groundswell*, authored by Charlene Li and Josh Bernoff, defines a social trend in which people use technologies to get the things they need from each other, rather than from traditional institutions like corporations.[8] Li and Bernoff craft their argument in relation to online user profiles as demonstrated in Figure 1.1. The majority of users (70%) are listed as "spectators"—meaning they use social media sites as a viable source of information. "Spectators" solicit the opinions of their friends via Facebook prior to making a purchase rather than consulting a company's site. This

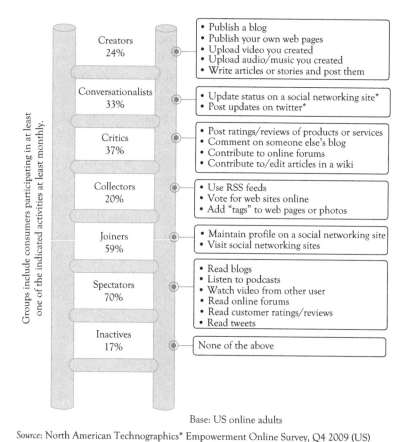

Base: US online adults

Source: North American Technographics* Empowerment Online Survey, Q4 2009 (US)
*Conversationalists participate in at least one of the indicated activities at least weekly.

56291   *Source:* Forrester Research, Inc.

Figure 1.1. The Lee-Bernoff model.

suggests that public relations and communication professionals need to monitor and embrace the "groundswell" to guide conversations, behaviors, and potentially gain some advantage in the social media territory.

PR Professionals as Social Media Experts

The burgeoning of conversation in the social media environment has created opportunities to position public relations and communication professionals as social media experts. After all, content creation has been the center of the profession throughout its history. Also, as PR professionals have become more active online, there is a new crop of social media-inspired roles, such as social media writers, bloggers, and strategists.

As of November 2010, Indeed.com, a search engine for jobs, reported postings with "social media" in the description tripled, reaching more than 14,000 in comparison to 4,300 postings in November 2009.[9] The site currently lists over 35,000 jobs with "social media" in its description.

The responsibilities for a social media role may include any of the following:

of BIL from in Uk

- Posting new content
- Managing the frontline by interacting with stakeholders (in real time)
- Initiating conversation to solicit feedback
- Seeking profile raising opportunities
- Overseeing digital initiatives

In these positions, public relations professionals are expected to possess advanced skills beyond the practical use of social networks. They need to have all the necessary qualifications to effectively curate an organization's brand identity, especially because of the substantial risks in the social media space.

As social media communicators, public relations professionals must

- be present,
- be actively engaged to influence conversations among stakeholders,
- deliver reliable information to people who consume goods and/or services,

- report findings to influence company decisions and policies,
- stay ahead of potential crises.

Overall, the social media expert must participate in deep social media engagement to better understand an organization's stakeholders' triggers/concerns and to anticipate/prepare a social media response, especially when the risks of an unfavorable response to an organization's policy changes and/or business decisions. This counseling role has become a critical competency for communications officers at the highest level.

Defining a Crisis

The Greeks called it "KRISIS," the moment of decision. The Chinese symbol

$$危机$$

is said to mean both "danger" and "opportunity." Both historic references imply decision-making at a turning point. What you decide to do, and to say, at these turning points determines your destiny one way or another. It drives whether you end up in danger or in opportunity. It is the place where reputations are won and lost.

Steven Fink, in his book *Crisis Management: Planning for the Inevitable*, asks four questions to define whether a particular situation is a crisis.[10]

1. Is this situation a precursor that risks escalating in intensity?
2. Does it risk coming under close scrutiny?
3. Will it interfere with normal business operations?
4. Will it jeopardize our public image or bottom line?

Answer those four questions positively, says Fink, and you have a crisis on your hands.

Steve Adubato, author of *What Were They Thinking? Crisis Communication, the Good, the Bad and the Totally Clueless*, defines a crisis as "...an out-of-the-norm problem, event or situation that cannot be handled through standard operating procedures."[11] Fred Garcia calls a crisis a "non-routine event that risks undesired visibility that in turn threatens reputational damage, operational disruption, or financial setback."[12] And, Don Stacks, Professor in the School of Communication at the University of Miami, says that crises fall into three general categories—physical, human, and managerial.[13]

> *Natural disasters* cause physical crises. Hurricanes, earthquakes, fires, and flood create crisis situations for the affected organizations. Technology failures are another way physical crises occur. Those would include mechanical failures, like the deadly gasses released at Union Carbide's Bhopal plant or the meltdown of the nuclear power plant at Chernobyl or, more recently, the failure of BP's Deep Horizon offshore oil rig.
>
> *Human behavior,* the second general category, includes both human confrontations and malevolence. Confrontations, often between NGOs and corporations, would include Nike's Asian labor crisis or Shell's ongoing issues with Greenpeace. In perhaps the most famous crisis in recent history, Johnson & Johnson faced deadly poison placed by an unknown assailant in its Tylenol packages. Corporate espionage, rumors, or the actions of employees would all fall within this category.
>
> *Management failures* often trigger crises. The decisions leading up to the Exxon Valdez's crash on the rocks off Alaska, the deceptive behavior of A.H. Robbins about the harmful effects of the Dalkon Shield, and the cigarette industry's failure to recognize and warn smokers of cancer risks all fall into the category of management failure. Management misdeeds—embezzlement, insider trading, sexual harassment—trigger crisis circumstances for the organizations they lead. Just look at Enron.

What Happens in a Crisis

For one thing, it is not pretty.

- A crisis overwhelms an organization's ability to conduct business. Everything stops until there is resolution.

- A crisis disrupts the organization's decision-making process. It isolates management until it is resolved. And then there's the pile-on effect. Regulators announce inquiries. Congress asks for testimony.
- Privacy gets stripped away in crisis. Every mistake that was ever made by the organization, no matter how long in the past, is dredged up and considered fair game. Memos to employees are instantly posted.

Suddenly, it is all personal. It is happening on your watch. It will define *you* as much as it defines the company. People caught in crisis are not necessarily thinking about what to do—they are wondering whether or not they will have a job in the morning. They think about how they will tell their wives or husbands. They wonder what their children will think of them. They think about the world they have carefully constructed over the past two or three decades crumbling before their eyes. And they try to come to grips with whether or not they are at fault.

If you are the person in charge, then to your various constituents and to the public, you are the person to hold responsible. You suddenly have a *credibility deficit* that hinders your ability to act. How can any one believe you can fix the problem if you were the one to cause it or allow it to happen?

Elizabeth Kubler-Ross created a model to explain the process that people go through when experiencing grief.[14] Following the death of a loved one, most people move through five mental stages: *Denial, anger, bargaining, depression,* and finally *acceptance*. People often behave this way in a crisis. Chief executive officers (CEOs) have been known to hide in their offices or in their travel schedules. Countless hours can be wasted on strategies that refute allegations. Assertions such as, "I am not a racist! I am not a harasser! You have the story wrong!" do little to promote solutions or restore credibility but are often the first instinct of business managers under fire. Ultimately, progress can only be made once acceptance is reached—acceptance that your credibility has been damaged, acceptance that stakeholders believe the allegations, acceptance that the allegations might be true, and acceptance that your first job is to restore the credibility lost often simply because of an association with that crisis.

Social Media and Crisis

In a social media-driven crisis, the elements of a traditional crisis are ever present. As in any crisis, a litmus test must be conducted to determine the opportunity, danger, and magnitude of response required to address an issue.

This new playbook still adheres to the basic principles of crisis management, but should be revised to include a social media response. In the event of a crisis, an organization's public relations and/or communications teams should be able to address stakeholders across multiple media platforms. For many audiences, social media is a first point of contact to receive breaking news.

Traditional news networks such as CNN, which has two verified twitter handles—@CNNBreakingNews with 9 million followers and @CNN with over 6.3 million followers—regularly provide announcements to their followers, as coverage streams across their websites and news stations. With that level of intense media scrutiny, concerned and impacted stakeholders are certain to log onto social media sites to initiate and partake in conversations that concern them. In comparison to traditional media, the use of social media has given stakeholders a more powerful voice to influence business/policy decisions that directly affect them. In times of crisis, stakeholders' use of social media has prompted the immediate response from organizations more than any other form of media, sometimes resulting in the increase in the damage already done or even creating a "crisis" out of what is actually a "non-crisis" by reacting too soon.

In a social media-driven crisis, organizations are exposed to the following additional risks:

- Increased negative conversation across social media platforms
- Traditional media interest
- Interruption of normal company operations.

According to Doorley and Garcia, "There is first-mover advantage in crisis response: whoever defines the crisis, the organization's motives, and its actions first tends to win. Silence on the part of a company is seen as indifference or guilt and allows critics, adversaries, the media, and the blogosphere to control the communication agenda."[15] Social media make gaining "first mover advantage" a tremendous challenge, as Glenn Engler, CEO of Digital Influence Group, asserts, "Consumers on social media are active, passionate, and demanding of transparency and engagement."[16]

Social media backlash to business and government decisions (e.g., Bank of America, Verizon, Hurricane Sandy, and the NY Marathon) is a direct result of the uncontrolled nature of its environment. Social media users have the benefits of direct access to wide audiences and transparency to express their disapproval about an organization's products, behavior, policies, and so forth. Consequently, people have free reign to discuss their opinions, whether positive or negative, at any given moment.

The "golden hour" in which a threat is first identified and possibly extinguished has become "golden minutes." Given the "instant nature" of social media, the period of response is reduced to the minutes for the time it takes a blogger to post an opposition piece or even the seconds it takes for a consumer to compose a 140-character tweet. The social media user now has the upper hand. "In the past, if a customer was dissatisfied with a product, they might write a letter or call the company directly, or tell a few people they knew. Now, those interactions are more likely to take place in the public square of social media for anyone to see, comment on, and spread even further."[17]

Blogs and consumer "fan" pages are a common location for users to express their dissatisfaction. The use of hashtags is an increasingly popular method for users to build threads of conversations surrounding a specific topic or issue on micro-blog sites such as Google+ and Twitter. Hashtags, while at times a valuable means for public relations and corporate communications to initiate conversations, can also produce a dangerous thread of negative commentary. McDonald's learned that the hard way. In early 2012, the fast food chain launched a promoted #McDStories on Twitter campaign to drum up positive stories about the brand. It was very quickly "hashtag-jacked" by Twitter users who used #McDStories to tell negative stories about the brand instead. Furthermore, with positive or negative momentum, a conversation can easily jump from one social network to another to become a trending topic across multiple social networking sites.

Once an issue reaches critical mass, it is fair to assume it will be picked up by traditional media outlets and replayed continuously in the 24-h news cycle, thereby allowing the tides to drastically shift against a company. The increasing backlash spread across multiple media platforms will in turn make it more difficult for public relations and communications practitioners to control the conversation in the midst of crisis.

Principles of Crisis Response

So given this reduction of response time, what should a public relations professional be prepared to do? There are several principles that the prepared communication professional should adhere to:

- *Lead, do not hide.* Joe Louis, the boxer once said, "You can run, but you can't hide." This is true in crises. While focusing blame may not be the answer, it is always a question. The more you duck responsibility, the more you hide, the more you lose credibility and are blamed.
- *Acknowledge the problem.* Even though you might not know much about the facts of the situation, even though you do not have a solution, you can at least acknowledge that there is a problem and say you are working on it. Do that right away.
- *Act in the public's interest.* Put more simply, "do the right thing." The public has an enormous ability to forgive if they perceive sincerity and concern in the organization's messaging. If stakeholders believe that your interests are the sole "Northern Star" for your actions, you will not be trusted with enacting a solution.
- *Move quickly.* Get to the bottom of a problem. Pose solutions. Define your own answers rather than have answers imposed upon you. Set the record straight. Delay gets confused with incompetence or simply not caring. Action, however small, builds confidence both internally and externally that progress can be made.
- *Fall back on your values.* Johnson & Johnson still gets credit for what may be the everlasting gold standard of crisis management.

When Tylenol capsules were tampered with and poisoned by a maniac, Johnson & Johnson did not hesitate for a minute. They withdrew the product everywhere. Their famous "Credo" was their guide in reacting to the Tylenol crisis. It starts with "…our first responsibility is to the doctors, nurses, and patients…" They never considered the bottom line. Follow J&J's fine example. Put your values ahead of your pocketbook.

- *Show compassion—apologize.* Care about the impact of the crisis on the people who are affected. Say you are sorry. People love to forgive and forget. Look at Bill Clinton, Tiger Woods, and Exxon.[18] You can be forgiven too.

- *Fix the problem.* Stop doing whatever is causing the harm. Do not do it again. And make it better. And do not forget; the cover-up is always worse than the crime. Every 10-year-old knows this. Most 40 year-olds have forgotten or suppressed it. Take a look at perhaps the best example in, Congressman Anthony Weiner's YouTube response as discussed in Chapter 4.[19]

- *Communicate fast and forthrightly.* Even before you fully understand the crisis, and well before you have a solution, you can still at least acknowledge that you know about the problem and that you are working on it. Talk east and walk east. Do not hedge, or use "weasel words," like President Clinton's attempt to ask what the meaning of "is" is.[20] And, do not cave in to the lawyers' demands for "no comment." Legal liability assertions are nonsense when your reputation is on the line.

- *Use all your channels.* It is time to employ all those channels you have built—Facebook, Twitter, YouTube, LinkedIn, blogs, your website, and so forth. And make sure the communication is appropriate to the channel.

- *Know when to take it offline.* A lot of customer service issues start with a simple question you can often answer with a phone call. Do not get into a back-and-forth argument online. Offer a phone number or email address. Even if it does not satisfy the person complaining, it at least shows others that you are trying.

Leading in a Social Media Crisis

Choosing a point person, the crisis leader, is a critical element in the process. The ideal candidates are experienced, decisive, and action-biased. They possess a high tolerance for ambiguity and enjoy solid credibility within the organization. Perhaps most importantly, they are courageous and thick-skinned. They need to be open to information, input, and feedback, and be able to take criticism well.

Crisis leaders must adhere to a strict code of ethics. They must accept accountability for their organization and for their own personal behavior. Honesty and transparency are keys. They must have a bias toward communicating and an appetite for quick response. Successful crisis leaders reduce the harm. They serve as a symbol of order and authority for their organizations. They provide reassurance to affected audiences and respond to their needs.

Contrast the outcome of a successful crisis leader, like J&J's legendary CEO Jim Burke, with the performance of Tony Hayward, CEO of British Petroleum. Burke's company faced the death of seven people. When he pulled the Tylenol from the shelves and championed reform in drug packaging, he became a hero and a legend. Hayward, by comparison, famously went to a sailboat race and was quoted as saying "I want my life back..." as his company spewed oil into the Gulf of Mexico. He lost his job over it.

Taking Control of the Communication

Some practical communications advice—not only do you need to know *who* is speaking for your company, you need to know *what tone of voice* they will use. Is it compassionate? Is it professional? Is it contrite? Is it combative? Each has its place depending on the type of crisis. Which do you use? Fight for your voice in the dialogue. If you can get one message inserted into the conversation, that is better than none. Two is better than one. Finally, *correct inaccuracies.* Watch the conversation and react in real time. Get your point of view inserted into the conversation in social media before the story has a chance to find its way onto a news broadcast or into print. Recognize the strengths and weaknesses of traditional and social media. Understand how they play off each other.

Recovery

You have to recover from a crisis in order to avoid reliving it. Define a process to prevent the crisis from happening again. Set milestones in delivering that process. Publicize the milestones, even if they are not newsworthy, because they demonstrate that progress is being made. Finally, do not hide your corporate social responsibility (CSR) initiatives under a basket. Be known for the good that you do in your communities, in the environment, in the workplace, and in the marketplace. Being a good corporate citizen is an essential component to protecting your corporate brand during a crisis. It is also the right thing to do.

Conclusion

The one thing to always remember during a crisis is that it is not about the issues. It is not about the recall or the lawsuit or the malfeasance or the oil spill or the plant explosion or the costs.

It is about credibility.

It is about your credibility—the credibility of your management to effectively manage, the credibility that you can handle the problem, and the credibility that it will not happen again. If you lose your credibility, and your stakeholders lose their confidence in you...you lose control over the crisis which means you have lost.

The tools have changed. The environment is hotter. But the defining question remains the same: "What are the reasonable expectations of stakeholders when something bad happens?" Answer that question right, and the rest is easy.

CHAPTER 2

Susan G. Komen's "Race for the Headlines"

Background

For 30 years, Susan G. Komen for the Cure symbolized, in action and behavior, the world's most powerful lobbying effort on behalf of breast cancer treatment, education, and research. Komen defiantly envisioned "a world without breast cancer" and set about to make that happen.

Since 1982, the Komen foundation has raised almost $2 billion dollars. Along the way, it created a network of 100,000 volunteers, sponsored the annual "Race for the Cure" events, and forged partnerships with corporate sponsors like Yoplait and Ford Motor Company. Komen also worked with groups like Planned Parenthood to provide better access to breast cancer screenings for low-income women. According to the non-profit's own website, 98% of women diagnosed with breast cancer today live at least 5 years. More than 75% of women over the age of 40 receive regular mammogram checkups.[1]

Pink power, as some have called it, is the result of founder and CEO Nancy Brinker's passion to do something "empowering" after her older sister, Susan, died of breast cancer. Susan Komen died of the disease shortly after being diagnosed with it in 1980. She was 36 years old. In a Washington Post profile, Nancy Brinker was described as warm, charming, and engaging.[2] She's also political. Brinker raised more than $100,000 for President George W. Bush's campaigns, earning the rare title of a Bush "pioneer." Along the way, Brinker forged a friendship with Karen Handel, who had unsuccessfully run for governor of Georgia.[3] Handel was a vocal opponent of Planned Parenthood and its funding of abortions.

In April 2011, Karen Handel joined Komen as the senior vice president of public policy, giving her a very powerful "seat at the table" within the organization. Her arrival set in motion a decision that would severely test and damage the organization's decades-long relationships with key stakeholders. Komen's downfall all started with a tweet.

The Crisis

On Tuesday, January 31, 2012, the Associated Press (AP) reported that Komen would no longer fund breast cancer screenings through Planned Parenthood.[4] Spokesperson Leslie Aun said the cutoff was the result of a governmental investigation of Planned Parenthood by U.S. House of Representatives Cliff Stearns, R-FL, over the possible use of public money to fund abortions. Komen board member John Raffaelli told the AP the board voted to require all vendors or grantees it supports to assert that they are not subject to any governmental investigations. Coincidentally, Planned Parenthood was the only grantee subject to an investigation.

Planned Parenthood was not happy about the Komen decision. The two had partnered since 2005. It was a loss of about $700,000 in breast cancer screening funding for low-income women, who are less likely to have mammograms because of financial constraints. Komen began discussing the idea of ending funding to its long time partner in October and by December its board voted to permanently sever ties.[5]

Planned Parenthood was ready and armed for a "street fight" with Komen, using social media as its weapon. Komen seemed to have no idea that it was about to get dragged into an instant social media crisis.

The Backlash

At 3:52 p.m., the same day of the Komen AP announcement, Planned Parenthood sent out the following tweet:

Planned Parenthood ✓
@PPact

Follow

ALERT: Susan G. Komen caves under anti-choice pressure, ends funding for breast cancer screenings at PP health centers
bit.ly/AloRdK

↩ Reply ↻ Retweet ★ Favorite

539
RETWEETS

17
FAVORITES

12:52 PM - 31 Jan 12 - Embed this Tweet

That tweet instantly activated an aggressive social media campaign that rallied Planned Parenthood's key stakeholders, influencers, and third-party advocates. Within hours, the print, broadcast, and online media were covering the rapidly unfolding social media crisis. Planned Parenthood spokespeople talked on TV, in the print, and online. Patrick Hurd, CEO of Planned Parenthood of Southern Virginia, told the Associated Press (AP), "Cancer doesn't care if you're pro-choice, anti-choice, progressive, conservative… victims of cancer could care less about people's politics."[6]

Twitter confirmed that from Tuesday evening through Friday afternoon, there were 1.3 million tweets posted about the Komen's decision. Komen became a trending topic. Facebook users changed their profile photos to protest the Komen's decision.[7] In the span of 72 hours, two of the most emotionally charged women's issues—breast cancer and abortion—were pitted against each other, and the loser was Komen. The organization minimally engaged with stakeholders on Twitter adopting a mostly defensive posture, while on Facebook it actually deleted negative comments from its page. *That is a big NO in social media.*

By Friday, Komen completely reversed its course and reinstated Planned Parenthood's funding. But the damage was substantial, to the brand, to its relationships with key stakeholders, and to its credibility as a non-partisan organization.

Komen's Mistake Chain

Komen made a series of key mistakes. They included inconsistency, poor delivery, transparency, hypocrisy, and a give-away of their power. These are fleshed out below and followed up a "lesson learned."

- *Inconsistency*—Komen flip-flopped on why it ended funding to Planned Parenthood. The reasons evolved from a government investigation to Planned Parenthood not performing the actual mammograms to Komen wanting to streamline the grant process.

  Lesson: Do not flip flop. Understand why a decision was made before announcing the decision.

- *Poor delivery*—Nancy Brinker did not deliver when she needed to. She failed to be the "warm, charming, and engaging" CEO when she needed to be during the crisis. Instead, Brinker appeared tense and defensive in an interview with Andrea Mitchell of NBC News and in a Komen-created video response posted on YouTube.[8] (Komen removed the video shortly after posting it on YouTube.) She violated the two "must have" behaviors of leadership during a crisis: do not be indifferent and do not be hypocritical.

Lesson: Delivery matters

- *Keeping insiders in the dark*—Key stakeholders, like volunteers, donors, researchers, the medical community, and even Planned Parenthood itself, learned about the decision from others. You do not do that to key stakeholders. Tell them first. People who are invested in an organization's success do not want to find out about a major policy shift from the news media. It is like breaking up with someone by changing the relationship status on your Facebook page to "single." It is a big No.

Lesson: Tell those who are closest to you first.

- *Huh?* On Friday, after an exhaustive 72 hours, Komen said, "Never Mind." No one likes getting jerked around, especially with a serious issue like breast cancer funding.

Lesson: Get it right the first time.

- *Hypocrisy*—It is not political, but it sure feels like it. Lower income women are less likely to receive health care, especially breast exams. Why cut off funding to the one group who benefits the most from it? The decision was confusing, hurtful, personal, and infuriating, words used over and over in various tweets and posts expressed on Twitter and Facebook. It was also not in keeping with the mission, vision, and values of Komen, whose actions contradicted its words.

Lesson: Stay true to your values.

- *Do not give away your power*— By not talking, by not clearly defining the issue, and by not *owning* it by being present and engaged with stakeholders, Komen allowed others to define its decision.

Lesson: Take control early.

Learning from Komen's Mistakes

Juxtapose Planned Parenthood's action with Komen's inaction. Komen was not prepared to handle the fallout on social media. It did not have a communication plan, nor did it have a social media strategy to explain its decision to stakeholders. This all took place in early 2012 when there was no excuse for not being prepared to talk and to engage on social media. So, what does this case teach us?

First, Komen's mistake is a lesson for all organizations: *be prepared with a comprehensive communication plan that includes a social media strategy*. Remember, if a decision has the potential to upset stakeholders, those groups are more likely now to voice their displeasure on social media sites. All it takes is one 140-character tweet to spark the fire.

Second, Stakeholders now expect symmetrical dialogues with organizations. Komen made a decision without consulting with or informing its stakeholders, many of whom supported the non-profit for decades. Instead, it let the Associated Press inform the very people who make up the backbone of its grassroots efforts. Komen would also not meet with Planned Parenthood, the key stakeholder in this, even after it reached out to the Komen board asking for a meeting about the decision.

Third, Komen was ill prepared to defend its major policy shift. It had no talking points to share, no assigned spokesperson, and no third-party advocates to defend its decision. During the critical "golden hour," Komen remained silent. Planned Parenthood owned the conversation and Komen's silence cost the once venerable organization dearly.

Fourth, they failed to understand that today's organization needs to react within minutes, not hours, after a crisis breaks. Social media compels them to. For an organization that spent years demanding that government, science, medicine, and people listen to them, Komen had nothing to say in a moment when it needed to say something the most.

The fallout continued after the funding was restored. Critics, media, and stakeholders began further scrutinizing Komen, including board members' salaries. There was renewed concern about "pink washing" because of the organization's efforts to "license" its iconic pink ribbon to fast food companies that, according to critics, promote unhealthy eating. Karen Handel resigned. In August 2012, Nancy Brinker stepped down as CEO.[9]

Ultimately, there are two vital lessons from the Komen crisis: (1) incorporate social media strategy into any crisis communication plan and (2) remember that stakeholders give a brand, a company, an organization, a person its power *and they can just as easily take that power away now using social media to do so*. There were a lot of stakeholders invested in Komen because the stakes were so high. While breast cancer is now treatable, it is not curable. One in eight women is still diagnosed with the disease today.

Parting Thoughts

Lou Says: How easy it is to be influenced by personal relationships. One of the biggest challenges leaders face is knowing who to listen to, and how to filter your personal feelings for someone from your business judgments. CEO Nancy Brinker failed to meet that challenge. She appointed her friend Karen Handel, a conservative politician, and then allowed Handel's personal views to affect the organization's non-partisan policies. The domino fallout created the crisis, cost Handel her job, cost Brinker her credibility, and cost Komen its reputation.

Susan Says: As I write this, I have a friend who is undergoing treatment for breast cancer right now. She's lost her hair, is battling extreme fatigue, and hoping the chemotherapy is worth the side effects. As women, we all know this disease intimately, either personally or through a friend, colleague, or relative. Lou and I first met when I enrolled his NYU crisis communication class that began, ironically, as the Komen crisis was unraveling. During one class discussion, I piped up that I thought Planned Parenthood had bullied the Susan G. Komen Foundation using aggressive social media tactics. Lou encouraged me to work through my gut reaction. I realized I was angry. Komen's efforts—fundraising, education, and lobbying—saved millions of lives.

They forced government to allocate resources to a "woman's" disease. I knew in my gut Komen's social media crisis would result in some permanent damage. And, it has. Almost a year after the crisis hit, Komen still struggled, according to The "New York Times" report on November 8, 2012.[10]

That's the power of social media today.

CHAPTER 3

#DearNetflix: I Am Cancelling My Subscription! Signed Social Media

Background

Marc Randolph and Reed Hastings co-founded Netflix in 1997. Headquartered in California, the company provides on-demand Internet streaming media and flat-rate DVD-by-mail services for movies and television.

The original business model was an online version of Blockbuster. You ordered a movie through its website, paid a one-time fee of $4 plus $2 in postage, and the DVD arrived in the mail. In 1999, Netflix introduced a monthly subscription and then discontinued offering single rentals a year later. The subscriptions offered unlimited rentals for a flat monthly fee. Netflix's service offered an appealing alternative to Blockbuster in which customers would have to get in their cars, drive to one of its stores to rent a DVD, drive home to watch it, and then drive back to return it within a certain time frame or face a late charge. With Netflix, customers could keep a DVD as long as they wanted. When they were ready to return it, the company enclosed a pre-paid envelope to put the DVD and pop it in the mail.

Twenty-four million customers flocked to Netflix because of that convenience, affordability, and an extensive online DVD library of movies, TV shows, and concert performances. With just a few keystrokes on their computers, people could order a movie that usually arrived in the mail the following day. Netflix had a well-oiled successful business operation with warehouses situated throughout the United States to respond immediately to customer requests.

The company went public in May 2002, selling 5.5 million shares at $15 per share. By July 2011, the price soared to $289 per share. By that time, Netflix was distributing over 1 million DVDs every day. Netflix was a public relations dream with intense customer loyalty, positive word of mouth reviews and the ability for friends to recommend movies to each other on their Netflix "Qs." It seemed nothing could stop the company's momentum.

The Crisis

On July 12, 2011, Netflix announced a 60% price increase and a plan to restructure its subscription plans into two separate plans.

> *Plan 1: Unlimited Streaming (no DVDs) for $7.99 a month*
> *Plan 2: Unlimited DVDs, 1 out at-a-time (no streaming), for $7.99 a month.*

This announcement came via the company's corporate blog,[1] and in an email to customers. It was greeted with a burst of negative reaction. Customers responded with anger and confusion and took to the social media to vent their frustrations. "I am shocked and appalled by your recent behavior," more than one person wrote on the Facebook page. People flooded Netflix's corporate blog with thousands of negative comments as well. On Twitter, the hashtag #DearNetflix became a trending topic and CEO Reed Hastings, on the receiving end of much of the wrath, earned the nickname GREED Hastings. The reactions on social media also attracted the attention of traditional news media outlets. Netflix's crisis was covered among all the networks and became a topic of discussion on financial news channel, CNBC.

Over the next 4 months, 800,000 people cancelled their subscriptions; stock price plummeted 77%. The company failed to do the number one thing in a crisis: *Respond Immediately.* As we will see with other case studies, companies that do not talk give others the opportunity to do the talking for them. In this case, the social media was responding—and very loudly. That mattered because social media now exert substantial influence on what news gets covered, how it gets framed during media coverage, and what perceptions lingered after the initial crisis hit.

The Response

On September 18, 2011, Netflix finally acknowledged the impact of its decision with a statement from Reed Hastings posted on the company's blog.[2] Hastings began by writing, "I messed up. I owe everyone an explanation." Only, Hastings did not really apologize. Instead, he announced yet ANOTHER set of business decisions that were changing Netflix's business structure even more. Hastings wrote the company would split the DVD and online-streaming plans into two different businesses. In his blog, he wrote that Netflix planned to rebrand its DVD rental service as an independent business/subsidiary company called Qwikster.

> It is clear from the feedback over the past two months that many members felt we lacked respect and humility in the way we announced the separation of DVD and streaming, and the price changes. That was certainly not our intent, and I offer my sincere apology. I'll try to explain how this happened... But now I see that given the huge changes we have been recently making, I should have personally given a full justification to our members of why we are separating DVD and streaming, and charging for both. It wouldn't have changed the price increase, but it would have been the right thing to do...It's hard for me to write this after over 10 years of mailing DVDs with pride, but we think it is necessary and best: In a few weeks, we will rename our DVD by mail service to "Qwikster."

Hastings' comments were not only poorly received, but ignited *another* instant social media crisis for the company. Stakeholders reacted to the newest announcement with another round of discussion, venting, and anger. The company blog post received almost 28,000 comments. Hastings followed that up with a very unpolished video statement in which he was seated next to the new Qwikster CEO Andy Rendich.[3] You can watch the amateurish video from a company in the video business (http://youtu.be/c8Tn8n5CIPk). Hastings even flubbed a line, repeating it again on camera. Let's just say the video did not build stakeholder's confidence in the Netflix management team.

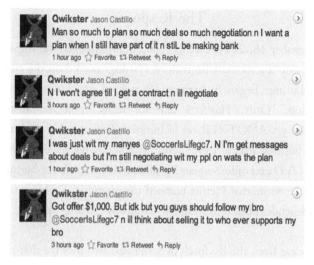

Figure 3.1. Twitter posts from Jason Castillo.

Ironically, while these additional business changes were being announced, the company created yet *another* crisis for itself (number 3). No one from Netflix bothered to confirm whether the Qwikster handle was available on all the major social media platforms, including Twitter. Sidebar: Always lock down social media handles before your company launched a product or business. Qwikster, it turned out, was already taken.[4] Its owner, Jason Castillo, was happy to part with the handle...for a price (see Figure 3.1).

In October 2011, Netflix announced it would reverse its decision to split the business but insisted on keeping the price change intact. Later that month, Netflix released another announcement stating more losses were expected in the fourth quarter of 2011. All the announcements only reinforced perceptions that the Netflix management was inefficient, indecisive, and completely disconnected from its customer expectations. By November 2011, the stock plummeted to $69, less than a quarter of its stock price at its high. Hastings paid a high price too. His compensation was cut by $1.5 million at the end of 2011 for the $12 billion mistake.

Chain of Mistakes

Companies make mistakes. The ones that handle them well recover from their crises quickly. Netflix clearly did not.

Some of Netflix's mistakes included:

- Mismanaged communication of the initial price increase.
- It did not do research to see how customers would react to a price increase.
- Timeliness of response: Netflix took *2 months* to address customer reactions to the price increase (July–September).
- CEO Reed Hastings never really apologized. Instead, he introduced yet another change to Netflix, Qwikster, when people were still upset over the initial changes.
- The welcome video on the Netflix blog introducing Qwikster's new CEO was vague, defensive, and unprofessional. Hastings said the video was created "to apologize in person, or on video, for something we did recently."[5] However, he never addressed the reason for the apology.

Effectiveness & Analysis of the Netflix Response

As Ken Chenault, CEO of American Express, said, "We have to remember that reputations are won or lost in a crisis."[6] Netflix's chain of mistakes led to a scarred reputation and an expensive business problem.

The threat from this type of crisis and the mishandling of the situation can have dire consequences, including a substantial drop in stock price, loss of business relationships, loss of customer subscriptions and/or demand of company products and services, reputational harm, and a lack in strategic focus as well as loss of confidence in company management. All qualify as *unintended but consequential impacts*.

Companies that take responsibility for their mistakes usually fare better than those that do not. In the age of social media, when customers are tweeting their anger and renouncing their subscriptions, the timing of response matters even more. As Professors Doorley and Garcia state, "The first determinant of success in protecting reputation in a crisis is the speed with which an organization reacts."[7] The media knows this too. As Ron Alsop, reporter for *The Wall Street Journal*, states, "crises aren't like fine wines; they don't improve with age."[8]

Netflix's response was neither timely nor effective. The company clearly failed to have a plan of action in place before addressing the problem. They did not anticipate the negative customer reactions, were unprepared to respond, and never looked at the problem from the customers' point of view. The stakeholders impacted by the crisis and its response included several of its key constituencies—customers, employees, and company shareholders. Netflix failed to address the concerns of these stakeholders, provided an insincere apology and, above all, failed to recognize the central problem. Netflix did not seem to understand that customers were not just unhappy that the price had increased, but were angry that the huge (60%) increase came without an explanation in the right context. (What was the benefit to/for the customer?) Especially during an economic recession, Nextfilx made a huge cut in entertainment and streaming options on the website with thin communication and no explanation.

Netflix relied on its customer loyalty during the initial phase of the crisis and assumed that customers would understand and still stand by the company. Eventually, Netflix did reverse its previous decision to separate into two businesses following customer reaction—finally a positive turnaround—but it still made no changes in the price increase. Hastings used social media platforms (blog and video) to announce a new change instead of using them to correct the company's first mistake. Unfortunately, he believed the problem revolved around his failure to *talk more* to his customers rather than *listen* to them. Ironically, one of the leading Internet pioneers seemed to not understand the principle rule of social media—it is about a *conversation*.

How Could Netflix Have Been More Effective?

When trying to determine whether a company is in crisis mode or not, it is important to answer certain questions. Some of the questions Garcia recommends asking include:[9]

- Does this situation/event risk undesired visibility?
- Would that undesired visibility threaten reputation damage and/or financial setback?
- What are the expectations of our stakeholders? (Do they expect us to do or say something now?)

- Will silence be seen as an indifference to the harm caused by the crisis?
- Are others speaking about us right now and what is the perception—negative or positive comments?
- Will we lose the ability to control the outcome if we wait any longer?

In the case with Netflix, the answer to all questions above was "YES," which means they were in a crisis and needed to accept their mistake and respond immediately. The company should have focused all its resources on fixing the problem and assuring its customers that it was "listening" and acting in beneficial ways for the customers. Netflix failed to frame the price increase to benefit the customer. The company underestimated the reactions, needs, concerns, and issues of the customer. There are always options available to avert a crisis—it just depends on what the company or individual chooses and the timing of the solution.

Ironically, Hastings' decision to change the business model was rooted in a solid business judgment. There is an inherent risk to change, especially when the "current" successful business model works. But, there is more risk in being left behind when technology is moving forward. Hastings' instincts were correct, but they were communicated poorly to stakeholders. Netflix saw a shift in the streaming business and thought that given the changing landscape of technology, it was time the company climbed the ladder. While Hastings did not have bad intentions, he took the customers for granted and assumed that a detailed, transparent, and clear explanation of the new business model was unnecessary. Hastings said in an interview with The Associated Press,[10]

We became a symbol of the evil, greedy corporation. Then we faced a reputational hit that created significantly more cancellation than we anticipated.

Netflix did not seem to realize that as far as customers are concerned, emotions trump facts, which is why the customers did not care about the business rationale behind the price increase. Even though Netflix did try to take action and respond to its customer concerns, it did so ineffectively and in a delayed manner. It came across as unprepared and scrambled to fix the problem. Netflix should have done *more*. Some actions it could have taken to fix the problem are as follows:

- *Sincerity*—Issue another apology, and a *real one* (within days of noticing negative comments/coverage) video on its corporate website and on YouTube and should have included the following:
  - Recognize the problem (price increase and lack of streaming options).
  - Explain why the problem occurred in the first place.
  - Apologize for the bad judgment, express embarrassment, and assure customers that immediate measures are being taken to remediate the problem.
- *Consultation*—Ask for customer input and the participation of stakeholders to help fix the problem, and avoid further problems in the future.
  - Increase online-streaming options and explain how the price increase related to securing additional media content for customers.
  - Use social media platforms such as Facebook, Twitter (where most of the negative comments were generating) to respond to individual customer concerns and/or direct them to the corporate website for more information on the change.
- *Customer involvement*—Since Netflix is so active on blogs, it should have used that as a platform to ask for customer feedback on the changes—"We as a company are thinking of doing this, what do you guys think about this plan?"

To conclude, Netflix handled the crisis quite poorly. Did it try to fix the problem? Yes, it did but not in a timely or effective manner. Could it have avoided the problem all together? Yes. It absolutely could have avoided the crisis if the company paid attention to the negative feedback in the initial phase. The company's delayed response allowed the media and public to frame the crisis, while the insincere apology only helped amplify the problem further. Netflix did do one thing correctly when it comes to social media: *It did not delete the negative comments off its blog.* We applaud them for that. We just wish they had read them.

In the long run, Netflix survives for now. But it is a company that is still perceived as having lost its way. Its stock price hovered around $69, a long way from its once high of over $200 a share. In late 2012, it also defended itself from a possible hostile takeover by activist investor Carl Icahn who revealed he owned 10% in the company. Netflix still has more than 27 million streaming members in the United States, Canada, Latin America, the United Kingdom, and Ireland.

Parting Thoughts

Lou Says: This is a classic case. Wouldn't you think that a technology leader like Netflix would have been able to plan and implement changes to its service without provoking an eruption of criticism and complaints in social media? It just goes to show how important planning, research, and careful implementation are in this conversation age. I've worked with a lot of CEOs, but this guy takes the cake. I'd have to agree with Vanity Fair. The magazine called the Netflix crisis the most self-inflicted crisis on an organization since New Coke.[11]

This story ought to worry every CEO. If Netflix can get it wrong, anybody can. After all, Hastings was named Fortune Magazine's Businessperson of the year in 2010.[12] And, to his credit, what he wanted to do made sense. The DVD's best days are behind it. Video streamed via the Internet is slowly replacing the physical disc, and betting a business on a dying product is never a great idea. So Hastings wanted to get ahead of the curve and focus on streaming, to disrupt his own business before someone else did it for him. It was aggressive, far-sighted, and very much in character.

But he forgot some important factors as he implemented this smart decision. Customers don't like change, and instead of explaining to customers why the change made *sense for Netflix*, Hastings should have explained why it made sense *for its customers*. It looks to me that while he was trying to take the company forward, his team put together a lousy communication plan and didn't anticipate the outrage on social media. He should have noticed.

Even when he finally got around to dealing with the outrage, Hasting's apology via the corporate blog was not well received, even though he finally tried to provide reasoning behind the company's decision to split the business and increase the monthly price. The apology came across as vague and superficial. While this may seem like nit picking, Hastings apologized for the fact that the *customer felt* mistreated instead of accepting that the company itself had mistreated them. In other words, this served as a "non-apology apology," where Netflix apologized but also claimed to be a victim itself. (*"I am sorry you feel that way"*...not *"I'm sorry I did it!"*). We all know how annoying when people we love do this—we aren't any happier when a company executive does it.

Susan Says: When CEO Reed Hastings made the decision to address the crisis on camera, he and his colleague reminded me of the "Wayne's World" skit from "Saturday Night Live." The two were seated outside with an odd background (Wait, is that a swimming pool? Um, is that the company parking lot? Why is Hastings dressed like Don Johnson from the 1980s TV Show "Miami Vice"?) See what just happened there. Don't let distractions distract from the message. That set-up looked amateurish, unprofessional, and unpolished. Coming from a TV background, I am always amazed at how multi-million dollar (heck, even multi-billion dollar companies) go cheap when it matters the most: putting their CEO on camera. Those details—how the CEO is dressed, the location, the lighting, how the CEO looks—matter. After all, you only have one chance to make a first impression. Netflix was a company in crisis by the time this video was made. Bring in a professional crew to stage, light, and videotape Hastings. Spend the money. That video was uploaded to YouTube where it was viewed thousands of times. Remember, thanks to smart phones, video can be easily accessed and watched on the social media today. So, if you are going to do a video response, I beg you please make sure it isn't slapped together and your CEO isn't dressed like it is 1985. I would have put Hastings indoors, in front of a neutral background with the Netflix logo, and I would have had him wear a suit. If you are a CEO, dress the part. It will inspire confidence among your stakeholders. Speaking of "Saturday Night

Live," it had its own take on the Netflix crisis. Lou and I agree it's never a good thing to get spoofed on SNL. I am amazed SNL found a shirt the same color as the one Reed Hastings wore in the video.[13] (To see this video, please go to http://www.nbc.com/saturday-night-live/video/netflix-apology/1359563/).

CHAPTER 4

To Tweet or Not to Tweet?

Background

Twitter has been described by many (these authors included) as the "wild, wild west" of social media. Since its March 2006 inception, Twitter has generated millions of daily tweets.[1] No fact checking or sourcing is required before a user tweets. There are no rules, no moderators to oversee trending topics or discussions among users. Users moderate each other. Tweets fall under the constitutional umbrella of freedom of speech. Rumors spread quickly. Celebrity deaths are among the most consistent and persistent falsities. In December 2011, Jon Bon Jovi reacted to Twitter chatter he had died of a heart attack by tweeting this photo.

Twitter:

Bon Jovi @BonJovi   19 Dec

"Heaven looks a lot like New Jersey" -jbj. Rest assured that Jon is fine! This photo was just taken. .fb.me/1uX5xLzSh

View photo

Facebook:

(https://www.facebook.com/photo.php?pid=8835959&l=d39bc9b4a2&id =7220821999 Photo courtesy: David Bergman, www.davidbergman.net)

Even after the photo share, some on Twitter disavowed the photo's authenticity, saying it looked photo shopped. Twitter is like that. You will not always be able to control the reaction, but you should try to control conversations about yourself and your brand.

In just a few years, Twitter has acquired more than 500 million active global users.[2] In 2010, Twitter played an integral role in the information dissemination of the Arab Spring uprising, the Japanese tsunami, and the earthquake in Haiti. The 2012 U.S. Presidential election became the first "social media" election with the candidates and their staffs using Twitter to actively engage with voters. The @BarackObama 2012 Campaign account generated over 7,000 tweets during the year. Even the President of the United States, Barack Obama, personally tweeted, signing his tweets with a "–bo."[3]

Example of –bo:

Twitter verifies accounts, like the President of the United States with the "coveted" blue check mark of authenticity. Stakeholders— whether fans, customers, or constituents—seek out engagement with those verified accounts more and more.

So, it intuitively seems to make good sense for high-profile people to be active on social media. It allows for a unique level of timely engagement. As of the writing of this book, Lady Gaga has over 31 million followers on Twitter. Teen heartthrob Justin Bieber follows closely behind with almost 31 million followers. Even the Speaker of the House, John Boehner, R-OH, is on Twitter with almost 400,000 followers. But, that level of engagement can come at a cost. Here we are talking about reputational damage to a brand. An ill-conceived, poorly worded 140-character tweet can do just as much reputational damage to an individual's image as a negative expose, news article, or smear campaign.

Twitter has been the source of some legendary "tweet in the mouth" social media crises for public figures, including former New York

Congressman Anthony Weiner and actor Ashton Kutcher. These *self-inflicted crises* arose out of a failure to grasp the larger impact of a tweet on reputation and image. When you are famous, there is always someone monitoring your Twitter account, waiting for that one tweet that will create an instant crisis for you.

It has become the modern social media twist on the age-old Shakespearean question: *To Tweet or not to Tweet?* To explore such self-inflected crises we turn first to U.S. Congressman Anthony Weiner (Democrat, New York) and then actor Ashton Kutcher, both of whose "star" status was negatively impacted by an inappropriate or wrong Tweet.

Anthony Weiner

Background. *Do not lie.* The cover-up is always worse than the crime. U.S. Congressman Anthony Weiner, presumably a student of history, should have learned those lessons from President Clinton and others. However, this self-inflected crisis was due to exactly that: Lying about something (a lewd photo sent from his personal Twitter account) and then trying to cover it up.

It was never going to be an easy crisis to navigate for the Congressman and his staff. Any crisis that has a sexual component attached to it begets additional communication challenges. But, Anthony Weiner violated the number one rule of any crisis, transparency. *He was caught lying.* As crisis expert Garcia notes, "the cover-up is always worse than the crime. Every 12-year-old knows this, but most-40 year-olds have either forgotten or suppressed it."[4]

In the span of 3 weeks, the seven-term Democrat from New York sunk from being his party's rising star to being unemployed. All because of lewd photos he tweeted to several women. Did we mention Weiner was married? His wife, Huma Adedin, was at the time pregnant and an advisor to then Secretary of State Hillary Clinton.

Chain of Mistakes. The social media crisis developed at whiplash speed. The timeline according to *New York Times* reporting covers 11 days:[5]

Friday, May 27, 2011: a lewd photo of an unidentifiable man in tight fitting underwear is sent to a young woman from Weiner's Twitter account. The photo is quickly deleted.

Saturday, May 28: a Twitter user discovers the photograph, shares it with his followers and conservative blogger, Andrew Breitbart. Breitbart's website, www.biggovernment.com, publishes the photo.

Saturday, May 28–Tuesday, May 31: Weiner denies he sent the photo. He and his staff spend the next few days telling media his Twitter account was hacked.

Wednesday, June 1: Weiner tells MSNBC he cannot "say with certitude" that it is not him in the photo.

Monday, June 6: Briebart publishes additional photos and emails sent by Weiner to women. During a press conference, Weiner admits he sent the May 27 photo and confirms it's him in the photo too. He also admits to inappropriate social media contact with additional women. He refuses to resign and promises to get help for his inappropriate behavior.

By old crisis standards, Weiner stumbled at first with lies and distractions, but he finally followed the rule book on effective crisis communication: *admit you are wrong, say you are sorry, do not do it again, and make amends.*

But, this was a social media created and fueled crisis. The rules are different. Because of the social media, Weiner's crisis got beyond him and his staff. Twitter was abuzz about this for days, with #Weiner #Weinergate and even #HumaAbedin trending. (Trending topics are the most popular tweeted subjects searchable by hashtags.) Media and culture influencer, The Daily Show host Jon Stewart, relished the comedic fodder offered at the Congressman's expense. Stewart even dubbed the social media crisis, "The Wangover," as a nod to the popular 2009 movie, "The Hangover," on June 8 and again on June13 as a two part parody of the bumbling politician.[6]

Weiner thought he could survive his social media crisis by employing crisis communication skills developed for *traditional* media responses. But, he took too long to come around to the truth. In the meantime, others defined it for him. He ignored the new reality created by the social media, and the new rules of the game: analysis, action, and communication all at high speed. His key stakeholders, Congressional colleagues and voters, viewed his reputation as broken beyond repair. And, on June 16, 2011, Anthony Weiner announced his resignation.

Ashton Kutcher

Background. *Know the facts before you tweet*. Simple enough, but it seems hard to do for some celebrities, even those who are accomplished social media users.

It was surprising, therefore, to find actor Ashton Kutcher involved in a social media crisis, given that he was an early and successful adaptor to Twitter. Kutcher was a prolific tweeter and the first celebrity to reach one million followers. The crisis involved legendary Penn State college football coach Joe Paterno, who had been caught up in another crisis situation not of his making. His social media crisis was short-lived; but, he could have avoided it altogether had he taken the time to learn the facts before hitting send on this tweet:[7]

How do you fire Jo Pa? #insult #noclass as a Hawkeye fan I find it in poor taste

The response to Kutcher on Twitter was immediate and overwhelmingly negative. Football Coach Joe Paterno had been fired from his long-time coaching position because of his connection to the unfolding Penn State child sex abuse scandal. Various media outlets had reported extensively on the scandal, Jerry Sandusky (the long-time child sex abuser), and Joe Paterno in the weeks leading up to the university's decision to relieve Paterno of his coaching duties. Kutcher is clearly a smart guy so it was baffling why he did not connect the dots, which is why we are including his social media crisis in this chapter. It is important to understand the context of a news event before you comment on it, especially as a celebrity. The Penn State sex abuse scandal was one of the top stories in search popularity during 2012.[8] There was a lot of anger directed at Paterno in particular.

Chain of Mistakes. Kutcher tried to fix his mistake by tweeting:

Heard Joe was fired, fully recant previous tweet! Didn't have full story
#admitwhenYoumakemistakes.

But, by that point, it was too late. The actor *deleted* his controversial tweets (a big no-no in Twitter best practices) and then tweeted this apology:

As an advocate in the fight against child sexual exploitation, I could not be more remorseful for all involved in the Penn St. case

His apology still wasn't enough. #AstonKutcher remained a trending topic. Trending topics for public figures are rarely for good reasons— either they have died or done something inappropriate.

Kutcher announced he was handing his account over to his publicity team to manage. It was an unfortunate end for a celebrity who had such a celebrated beginning on Twitter.

Lessons Learned. Tweets, like anything posted online, live forever. We live in a 24/7 society now where social media platforms, particularly Twitter, are *always* active. If you are a public official or celebrity and you tweet something controversial it has likely been screen grabbed, re-tweeted, and extensively reported on before you have a chance to delete it. TMZ, the celebrity news website, spends a great deal of time reporting on social media induced crises created by celebrities and public figures.[9]

If you have a smart offensive strategy on Twitter, you will be less likely to need a defensive one. Ask what are the mission, strategy, goals, and tactics for the "personality" you are representing? Is the entertainer or public official promoting specific projects him- or herself or using the social media as a means of personal expression? Be *transparent* about that with Twitter and other social media followers. Make a candid evaluation of your social media objectives. Weigh the risks and rewards involved. It is also a good idea to have a social media team or person who can vet tweets before they go out.

The appealing quandary about Twitter is it allows "personalities" to directly tweet with their audiences. But, that direct engagement involves a fair amount of risk, as we saw with Ashton Kutcher.

One of the biggest complaints, after Ashton Kutcher announced he would no longer personally tweet, was the loss of Kutcher's authentic voice. It is a delicate balancing act when you engage on social media—between being authentic and keeping it a little "too real" with your personalities' followers.

We cannot stress this enough: *think before you tweet*. If you have a tweet you are unsure about, do not send it. Walk away from that laptop. Put the smart phone down. Clear your mind. Ask yourself, is this tweet appropriate? Is it factually correct? Is it fair? Will it hurt or help my image? Something as simple as a 140-character can be a loaded weapon in the wrong hands.

Get educated. Ashton Kutcher tweeted out a defense of Joe Paterno without first getting the context of why Paterno was let go. Find out *why* something is trending on Twitter. Go to a neutral, traditional news source to confirm the information before you take a stand on it. Also, check out the trending topics; click on the hashtag to see what people are saying about the topic.

Here are some other takeaways:

- Do not engage in sexually explicit behavior on social media. Learn from Anthony Weiner. It will not end well. The media and the public will also have no sympathy, wondering why you did not learn from Anthony Weiner.
- Everybody is looking for his or her 15 min of fame (hat tip to Andy Warhol). If you are famous and you direct message someone on Twitter, it will not stay private long. Trust us.
- George Orwell was right.[10] If you are a public official, particularly an elected official, your "enemies" are monitoring your online activity. All the time.
- Before you tweet, do your own movie rating on it. Ask yourself: Is this tweet G, PG, or R rated? Will I embarrass my family and friends? Do my followers want these kinds of tweets from me?

- Ask yourself will my tweet help, hurt, or have a neutral impact on the brand of *me*. Will it draw unnecessary attention?
- Do not email when you are angry. Same advice applies to tweeting. Trust us. It does not end well, especially when you are a "personality."
- Do not participate in rumormongering. Director Spike Lee tweeted out the Florida address of George Zimmerman, the man accused of the 2012 racially motivated shooting of unarmed 17-year-old black teenager Trayvon Martin.[11] The only problem? Lee reported the wrong address—it was not Zimmerman's address but an elderly couple unaffiliated with the story. They fled their home in fear because of Lee's tweet.
- The Spike Lee mistake is also a reminder that as a public figure your tweets carry more weight among the Twitter community. Be informed. Ashton Kutcher learned that lesson. So did Reality TV star Kim Kardashian.[12] In January 2012, she tweeted the following:

Did I juist hear Cher has passed away? Is this real? OMG

It was another celebrity death rumor. But, because her tweet reached her millions of followers, the rumor only gained steam. Cher ultimately took to Twitter to squash it much like Jon Bon Jovi did.

- Which brings us to our next suggestion: do not react or put out a tweet about a famous person's death until a spokesperson has actually confirmed it.
- Do tweet if it will help neutralize a potential crisis. During a 2012 Republican debate, Texas Governor Rick Perry, a presidential candidate (albeit very briefly), forgot the name of one of the agencies he promised to eliminate.[13] Rather than let Twitter define (and make light) of his mistake, Perry took ownership of it by tweeting out the following:

Rick Perry ✓
@GovernorPerry

Really glad I wore my boots 2nite because I stepped in it out there. I did still name 2 agencies to eliminate. Obama has never done that!

Sometimes, a sense of humor is the best way to score points on Twitter or, at least, get users to leave you alone.

- Our last piece of advice: use correct grammar and proper spelling when tweeting. Your image will only improve when you know the difference between You're and Your. Trust us.

Looking Ahead

Twitter will continue to be a dominating presence on the social media landscape. People, these authors included, now watch TV events, like the Olympics or the U.S. Presidential debates, with an accompanying laptop or smart phone tracking the real-time reactions on Twitter. The microblogging site has become *that* influential.

We believe part of media training for any public personality or official must include social media training, especially *engagement* on Twitter. We expect there will continue to be social media crises involving the famous. Many of those crises will likely implode on Twitter. But, we hope none will involve unseemly photos of underwear.

Parting Thoughts

Lou says: Sometimes I look at the behavior of high-profile people and wonder, "How could anybody be that dumb?" Does their ego cloud their judgment? Do they think they can get away with it because they're special? My best advice is to use a sounding board. When I was running MS&L my communications director, Dierdre Dapice, looked at every email I sent, especially when I was upset. She often said, "I hope you feel better, now delete it!" She saved me a lot of trouble. Everybody needs a Dierdre.

Susan says: As a former journalist, I have a litmus test for the famous and their crises. I ask, "will it make the person's obituary?" It's a sobering way to assess the long-term fallout. For all of former President Bill Clinton's achievements, his impeachment will still be in paragraph one in his *New York Times* obituary. Anthony Weiner's inappropriate Twitter behavior cost him his Congressional seat and will guarantee a mention in his obituary as well. Remind your clients their bad behavior on social media has the potential to haunt them for eternity.

CHAPTER 5

Bank of America Stands Down

There was a time not so long ago when banks had a clear and defined upper hand over the customers who did business with them. Banks talked at their customers with classic asymmetrical (one-way) communication, and they liked the relationship they defined by those parameters.

That, of course, was before social media.

If you learn nothing else from this book, learn this: *social media has changed everything when it comes to communication between businesses and the people they serve.* Banks are no exception. Some, like Wells Fargo and Chase, have embraced social media. Others, like Bank of America, learned the hard way that the era of the asymmetrical conversation is over.

Background

In 2011, Bank of America (B of A) made a business decision to impose a fee on its debit card users.[1] Customers responded, channeling their own Howard Beale moment from the 1976 movie, "Network" (http://www.youtube.com/watch?v=dib2-HBsF08). Customers were "mad as hell" and they took to social media to express it. Bank of America was ill prepared (some, like these authors, might argue it was arrogant) about the social media crisis that hit them. But, make no mistake; this crisis hit them hard, humbling the banking colossus.

With over 12% of all bank deposits in the United States, Bank of America stands as giant among American multinational banking and financial service organizations. Headquartered in Charlotte, North Carolina, it is considered the nation's largest bank by deposits, and the fifth-largest company overall in the United States. It boasts serving 99% of the Fortune 500 companies, and its retail banks cover more than 80% of the U.S. population.

In recent years, Bank of America has been plagued with controversy following a series of missteps in the wake of the 2008 economic downturn. Its purchase of Merrill Lynch saved the giant brokerage firm from bankruptcy, but generated a wave of troubles for the bank. Massive trading losses were revealed, the management team at Merrill left, and in the end the Federal Government intervened to force B of A to complete the deal.

As a result of the Merrill acquisition, the bank needed a Federal bailout. It received $18 billion in the fall of 2008, and another $20 billion in January 2009 from the Federal Troubled Asset Relief Program, known as TARP. But things just kept getting worse. In August of 2009, the bank agreed to pay a $33 million fine to the Securities and Exchange Commission because it had not disclosed an agreement to pay billions in bonuses at Merrill Lynch. A month later, a federal judge rejected the settlement and threatened to take the case to trial. Ultimately, the case was settled for $150 million.

With the American economy in crisis, the federal government took action. President Obama signed the Dodd-Frank Wall Street Reform and Consumer Protection act[2] into law in July 2010. A complex bill, it greatly increased regulatory scrutiny of U.S. financial institutions.

The Durbin Amendment was a key provision of the bill.[3] It regulates the interchange fees large banks can charge retailers to process transactions and gave the Federal Reserve the authority to set those fees. At the end of June 2011, The Fed cut the fees dramatically. The new structure capped bank fees to merchants for processing debit card transactions at 21 cents per transaction from an average of 44 cents. The 23 cent reduction per transaction translates to an estimated $6.6 billion loss in revenue for the financial services industry.

Three months after this announcement, Bank of America made a head-shaking business decision which appeared to be devoid of any consideration for customers or the two federal bailouts it had received just a few years earlier. And, it created a social media crisis and then handled it in the worst possible way: its CEO got defensive.

The Crisis

On September 29, 2011, a few weeks after the government cap was put in place, Bank of America announced plans to institute a $5 monthly usage fee for its debit card. It offered no explanation for the new fee.[4] The new fee was a less than oblique attempt to transfer the potential loss in revenue from its merchants directly to its retail consumers.

Now, just consider for a moment the effect of Bank of America's actions from the customers' point of view. In those strained economic times, where the average American was been personally impacted by the financial collapse of 2008, money was tight. A $5 charge was significant, especially when the service was previously free. And, it came on the heels of Congressional action that was supposed to save banking customers money. Coincidence? Definitely not, judging by the comments on social media.[5]

Customers reacted quickly and emotionally to B of A's announcement, turning to the social media to vent frustrations. It also did not help that the media coverage related to the debit fee charge followed the bank's September 12th announcement of plans to eliminate 30,000 jobs.

Public Response

In a world where "reputation is all you have" and "perception is everything," a company's ability to survive is dependent upon its relationships with its stakeholders. The proliferation of the social media and evolution of the 24-hour news cycle allow the tides to drastically shift against a company in the minutes it takes a news organization to produce a story or a blogger to post an opposition piece.

According to Twitter, there were thousands of tweets within 24 hours of Bank of America's news protesting the fee add on.[6] Mainstream media jumped in immediately to report on the backlash reverberating among the different social media platforms. The media focused its attention on one young woman who took protesting to a new "social" level with her anger against her bank.

One day after Bank of America announced the new debit fee, Molly Katchpole, a 22-year-old Bank of America customer, harnessed the power of people in an entirely new social way. She formed a grassroots campaign and online petition using www.change.org to call attention to the bank's move. Change.org describes itself as a social action platform that empowers anyone, anywhere to change the world. In 2 days, her site registered 125,000 signatures.[7] Within a month, her site registered 300,000 signatures.

Katchpole, who was young and well spoken, became the "face" of the campaign and an instant media darling. On broadcast after broadcast, print interview after print interview, Molly shared her story of struggling to get by in these lean times. Her personal narrative—a recent college graduate working two part-time jobs to make ends meet on a tight budget—dovetailed nicely with the media's portrayal of the B of A move as nothing more than ugly corporate greed taking advantage of people who are financially struggling to survive in these tough economic times.[8] Katchpole's story inspired other citizens to follow suit, posting videos on YouTube, and other social media platforms (see, for example: http://www.youtube.com/watch?v=rxKuAGMrmqM). The negative coverage on the Internet fed the mainstream media cycle, which allowed for heighted exposure among various audiences. Traditional media outlets closely followed the social media response and found other "Mollys" to speak about their financial hardships and disdain for the bank too.

The Bank's Response

In the days following the announcement and subsequent backlash, Bank of America leadership remained steadfast in its decision to charge customers fees and refused to engage the media and public. A full week went by before Brian Moynihan, the bank's president and CEO, emerged in an interview with CNBC, to say, "we have a right to make a profit."[9]

Later, speaking with ABC News, he stated the additional fees would allow the bank to provide "great service" without any additional explanation of benefits to customers. In another interview, Bank of America Spokeswoman Anne Pace stated, "the economics of offering a debit card have changed with the recent regulations. As a result, we have decided to introduce a monthly usage fee."[10] Failing to address the public's concerns, both Moynihan and Pace's statements did not convince customers or protestors.

Resolution

On November 1, 2011, exactly a month after the announcement, Bank of America withdrew its plans for the debit usage fee.[11] The announcement came a day after the bank's competitors, Wells Fargo and JPMorgan, dropped their plans to levy similar charges, leaving the B of A as the last of the big banks pushing for the unpopular fee.

"We have listened to our customers very closely over the last few weeks and recognize their concern with our proposed debit usage fee," said David Darnell, co-chief operating officer in a press release, "Our customers' voices are most important to us. As a result, we are not currently charging the fee and will not be moving forward with any additional plans to do so."[12]

Further Fallout

An art gallery owner in Los Angeles named Kristen Christian was outraged by the Bank of America debacle. She built a Facebook page called "Bank Transfer Day" http://www.facebook.com/Nov.Fifth.[13] The site initially called for people to transfer their accounts from the large banks to credit unions, which are owned by the members. It drew more than 57,000 "likes" and continues as a popular gathering place for protests over bank activities.

Lessons Learned

Timing is everything. By making its announcement on the heels of the Durbin Amendment, Bank of America was looking for trouble. The new fee had people sarcastically asking, "Coincidence? I think not." The bank's motives were viewed as a greedy corporation's finesse of a government program aimed at saving and protecting consumers' money.

The other big lesson to come out of this: *understand the business, political and economic environments you operate in.* Yes, capitalism is about making money. Bank of America, however, made a pretty ruthless business decision on the heels of one of the worst economic downturns (some would argue the worst) in U.S. history. The $5 charge was seen as a big bump up for people who are barely making it, or who may be unemployed. There was little sympathy for banking and Wall Street after the 2008 market crashes.

And lastly, the Bank of America fiasco is proof that *before you act, you must think through a communications plan.*

- Do your research.
- Explain your business decisions to your stakeholders.

Bank of America offered no explanation for the fee, allowing customers to make assumptions in the days following the announcement. Considering all of the recent controversy and negative press coverage the bank had suffered, they should have been prepared to address stakeholders at the point of the announcement. In the Conversation Age, every business decision has to be evaluated in the context of the social media reaction that should be anticipated.

Bank of America violated *a key rule of crisis management, "lead, do not hide."* They should have engaged customers on the various social media platforms used to challenge the bank's position. The public today expects a two-way dialogue, not a brick wall. If they had explained themselves in a forthright and transparent way, they would have had a better chance to connect with the customers impacted by the fees. Lastly, the bank should have also issued an apology with its announcement to withdraw fees as an attempt to win favor with its publics. This crisis ended in favor of the customer, and left B of A with a long-lasting black eye.

Conclusion

Bank of America failed in both its actions and its communication. Their knee-jerk reaction to the regulatory changes never took the customer's point of view into account. Perhaps as a result of this experience, the bank now appears to be working on the development of a more vigorous dialog with its customers. It has built a Facebook page (http://www.facebook.com/BankofAmerica) and a Twitter account (https://twitter.com/BoA_Community) where it emphasizes its community support and corporate social responsibility (CSR) activities.

It has also developed programs to enhance the value of its credit and debit cards. Through a partnership with museums, zoos, and other cultural centers, the Bank offers free admission by showing its card.

But Bank of America faced a slow and long recovery process. More than a year after the debit card debacle, protestors still targeted the bank during the Democratic National Convention in Charlotte, NC.[14] The 60-story corporate headquarters there was a natural target, the tallest building between Philadelphia and Atlanta. CEO Brian Moynihan admitted months later that the $5 fee was a bad idea. "We struck a chord with customers that no one anticipated. We learned our lesson and stopped it."[15]

Time will tell how well those lessons have been learned.

Parting Comments

Lou says: CEO Brian Moynihan took "tell the truth" to a new low when he defended the $5 fee by saying "we have a right to make a profit." He failed to answer a basic question correctly—"What are the reasonable expectations of our stakeholders?" As a result, his credibility and the credibility of Bank of America were seriously damaged. In 2011, the bank appeared as number 141 on the Forbes reputation index of 150 biggest companies earning a slot on the list of "10 Least Reputable Big Companies."[16] A bank, "learning its lesson" about the power of social media in late 2011, ought to fire its communications staff.

Susan says: The social media dictates much of the editorial coverage by mainstream news organizations today. I attended daily editorial meetings where news coverage was outlined for the next broadcast. During my last few years, the senior editorial staff always asked what the social media hot topics were and what stories were generating the most views, most comments, and most shares on the news organizations' own websites. The Bank of America story is an example of one that played out long after the typical 24-h news cycle. In fact, B of A played out for over a week because of such a strong presence on multiple social media platforms.

PR professionals must remember that journalists love to report on "David versus Goliath" news stories, particularly in the aftermath of the financial collapse that left so many people jobless, homeless, and retirement accounts zeroed out. Many reporters view themselves as "Robin Hood" when it comes to covering the financial institutions in the wake of the 2008 economic collapse. That's why it's so important to have a communications plan, act on it immediately, and respect the power of the social media. As my writing partner, Lou, often warns: if organizations do not define themselves, others will do it for them. And, you do not want national news organizations listening to the others doing that defining.

CHAPTER 6

The Friendly Skies
Turn Ugly

Background

In 2011, an average of 1.73 million people in America took an airline flight every day, according to the Bureau of Transportation Statistics.[1] Customer service remains one of the hallmarks of the industry. From assisting customers with booking airline tickets to checking them in at the airport to providing them with safe, courteous service during a flight, airlines' reputations intrinsically link in to that service chain. If one link breaks, an airline's reputation can be damaged and its business left vulnerable. Airlines must make the flying experience as pleasant as possible, after all its business depends on repeat customers.

For decades, United Airlines enticed passengers with a siren call of "Fly the Friendly Skies." But in reality, United and other airlines cannot always make good on that tagline. Luggage gets damaged. Flights become delayed. Airplanes are more crowded. Then, there is always that crying baby on board. Lousy customer service can be the tipping point for the already frazzled passenger, the *key* stakeholder for any airline.

At one time, that unhappy passenger's only recourse was calling the airline's 1-800 number or writing a letter. Even an irate passenger ranting at an airline's service desk at the airport might get overheard by a few people at most. The social media have changed with whom and how those rants are heard.

Twitter, Facebook, and Instagram all serve as online repositories for unhappy airline service today. Get an attitude from a flight attendant? That passenger can instantly tweet his or her dissatisfaction. Imagine the power in that! Thanks to WIFI availability on most flights that tweet can go out even before the flight attendant has moved on to the next passenger row. Facing a delayed takeoff? Post your anger on Facebook. Luggage damaged during the flight? A photo posted to Instagram can visually express displeasure. While the social media are a win-win for the passengers, it is a big loss (and headache) for airlines' communication teams, who have to anticipate, navigate, and resolve the fallout from an angry tweet, post, or photo on social media.

In this chapter, we briefly examine four airline case studies where their crises played out in the social media. In 2011, JetBlue for a second time left passengers sitting on the tarmac for hours. Southwest Airlines had two high profile altercations with celebrities who took to Twitter to accuse the airline of discrimination. Finally, we look at a dispute between actor Alec Baldwin and American Airlines. Baldwin may have gotten to Twitter first, but American Airlines used the social media more effectively to respond and neutralize the situation, proving a crisis that begins on the social media can just as quickly end there too—if it's handled correctly.

JetBlues

Background

JetBlue is the relatively young (it was founded in 1998 by David Neeleman) airline known for its nonunion shop and affordable airfares. It quickly became the travel darling of jet-setting passengers by offering cool in-flight amenities like a TV on every seat. Wall Street embraced the airline too, the only one to turn a profit in the aftermath of 9-11. JetBlue had a business runway cleared for big expansion takeoff. Its company even created an advertisement campaign around the theme of "You Above All."[2]

But even TVs for every passenger do not protect an airline from a crisis. On February 14th, 2007, JetBlue infamously left passengers stranded on its airplane for 14 hours sitting on the runway at JFK Airport during a bad winter storm. The airline, to its credit, immediately activated best practice crisis management behaviors, including having CEO David Neeleman apologize and create a JetBlue *Customer Bill of Rights*.[3] The Bill of Rights set up a compensation program for flight delays to ensure that the extreme conditions passengers were subjected to, ironically enough on

Valentine's Day, would never happen again. CEO David Neeleman embarked on an aggressive media tour that included a videotaped apology posted on YouTube (http://youtu.be/-r_PIg7EAUw).[4]

The social media were still in its infancy, but JetBlue was praised for embracing it as a tool to reach its stakeholders. Everyone from JetBlue management to passengers to members of Congress assumed that terrible incident on the runway was an outlier never to be repeated again.

Unfortunately, it would be repeated less than 4 years later. This time the crisis was documented on social media as passengers trapped indefinitely onboard a JetBlue airplane provided real-time reports about their predicament, watched by everyone, including JetBlue.

The Crisis

We are shaking our heads as we write this but, once again, in October 2011, JetBlue held hundreds of passengers' hostage on their airplanes at the Hartford, Connecticut, airport. A freakish October snowstorm had forced the airline to divert six flights with 700 passengers. The Associated Press reported one JetBlue plane was held for 7 hours and the crew ran out of food, water, and the toilets stopped working. Passengers took to social media to let the world know about their predicament.

JetBlue passenger Andrew Carter tweeted:

Still on the plane. We haven't moved. Now EWR closed. Getting ugly in here. People yelling wanting to get off.[5]

In an email to reporters, JetBlue blamed the delays on a "confluence of events" caused the flight diversions and tarmac delays:[6]

Due to a confluence of events, including infrastructure issues in New York/JFK and Newark, JetBlue diverted 17 flights on Saturday. Six of those flights diverted to Hartford," the airline said in its e-mailed statement. "We worked with the airport to secure services, including remote deplaning and lav servicing. Obviously, we would have preferred deplaning much sooner than we did, but our flights were six of the 23 reported diversions into Hartford, including international flights. The airport experienced intermittent power outages, which made refueling and jet bridge deplaning difficult.... We have communicated directly with our customers impacted by this confluence of events to apologize as well as provide a full round trip refund, as it remains JetBlue's responsibility to not simply provide safe and secure travel, but a comfortable experience as well.

JetBlue's Chain of Mistakes

How did JetBlue let this happen again? The first step in crisis management is "fix the problem." The last is "make sure it never happens again." They know the critical role customer service plays in their success. Yet JetBlue, for a second time, failed at its customer service.

The airline waited a full day before it posted a statement on its website. It should have been monitoring Twitter and Facebook—and responding immediately. Clearly, the airline did not have continuous monitoring in place and/or had not empowered its monitors to respond to breaking events.

It also should have done more to compensate passengers who were held on the plane for so many hours. Refunding each ticket is the first step in making amends, not the only step. The airline also left stranded passengers to fend for themselves in Hartford after they were finally allowed to deplane. Going above and beyond the requirements of the situation is critical in a crisis.

Lessons Learned

It seems pretty simple. Do not keep passengers trapped on an airplane with no food, water, or working bathrooms for 1 hour, much less 7. And if, for some horrible reason you do, respond immediately and go the extra mile to make up for it.

Southwest: Heading SOUTH

Southwest Airlines, the Dallas, Texas, based airline, built a positive reputation for its quirky, independent spirit. It was known for affordable airfares and crews who sing during flight announcements. Its stock symbol on NYSE is LUV. Fortune Magazine consistently ranks it among the best for corporate reputation.[7]

Southwest proudly boasts it is LGBT (lesbian, gay, bisexual, and transgender) friendly. It also embraces the social media by tweeting and blogging. That is why the two case studies you are about to read are so puzzling. They are so an anathema to the image and brand Southwest spent decades shaping.

Background

It is a fact that airline seats are a little snug even if you are on the slender side. But, what if you are obese? Airlines are dealing with more and more overweight passengers as obesity numbers continue to climb in the United States. Airlines now have "customer of size" policies that require obese passengers to purchase an extra airline ticket if they are unable to put the arm rests down and sit comfortably in an airline seat. Airlines say this policy was created for safety concerns only.[8] Their argument is that if a passenger cannot buckle the seat belt and put the arm rests down, he or she is not safely secured for takeoff. That passenger might also be affecting the comfort level of adjacent passengers.

Yet, these policies are very subjective in nature. After all, how do you define comfortable? What if, like a size-too-small pair of jeans that you somehow manage to get on and buttoned up, the obese passenger can get the arm rests down and, with a seat belt extender, can get buckled up? What if a passenger does not want to or cannot afford to buy a second seat? With airlines aware that more passengers are overweight today, should they be offering wider seats? Is this a form of discrimination based on physical appearance? The "customer of size" policy was a crisis waiting to happen.

The First Crisis

Kevin Smith wears multiple hats in Hollywood—as a director, producer, actor, and writer. He has an intensely loyal following due to his breakthrough role as "Silent Bob" in the 1994 movie *CLERKS*. Smith regularly hosts podcasts and is actively engaged on social media. Smith's fans follow him, including on Twitter, where he has millions of followers.

He is also a very large man.

In 2010, Smith was overweight by his own admission. In February that year, he boarded a Southwest Airlines flight in Oakland for Burbank, California. Smith put his bag in the overhead compartment, put his seat belt on, and lowered the arm rests readying himself for takeoff. Instead, Smith was escorted off the plane after the flight Captain eyeballed him and deemed him too fat to fly.

Smith immediately and aggressively took to Twitter:[9]

"Dear @SouthwestAir-I know I'm fat, but was Captain Leysath really justified in throwing me off a flight for which I was already seated?

I'm way fat…But I'm not THERE just yet. But if I am, why wait til my bag is up, and I'm seated WITH ARM RESTS DOWN. In front of a packed plane with a bunch of folks who'd already I.d.ed me as "Silent Bob".

You (messed) with the wrong sedentary processed-foods eater.

I broke no regulation, offered no 'safety risk' (what was I gonna roll on a fellow passenger?)

Wanna tell me I'm too wide for the sky? Totally cool. But fair warning folks: IF YOU LOOK LIKE ME, YOU MAY BE EJECTED FROM SOUTHWEST AIR.

So, @SouthwestAir, go f*** yourself.

The SouthwestAir Diet. How it works: you're publicly shamed into a slimmer figure. Crying the weight right off has never been easier!

Even after Southwest put him on another flight Smith's tweet pummeling continued.[10]

"Hey @SouthwestAir! Look how fat I am on your plane! Quick! Throw me off!" (This tweet was accompanied by the photo at Figure 6.1)

Figure 6.1. Kevin Smith

Hey @SouthwestAir! I've landed in Burbank. Do not worry: wall of plane was opened & I was airlifted out while Richard Simmons supervised.

Southwest's Response. People rubberneck on the social media during a crisis, often watching it unfold in real-time. Many of those people are Southwest's key stakeholders—customers, employees, and stockholders. That is why businesses literally have minutes to respond before a potential crisis can spiral away from them like it did for Southwest.

#KevinSmith and #Southwest became trending topics on Twitter. That attention attracted coverage from news organizations, including ABC News, *The New York Times* and Entertainment Tonight. The National Association to Advance Fat Acceptance called for a boycott of the airline.[11] It got that bad that fast for Southwest. It had itself an instant social media crisis.

In fairness to Southwest, the airline did try to respond quickly, including aggressively on Twitter. There were at least eight tweets directed to Smith. It just did not do it very well. The first statement essentially blamed the victim embracing a passive-aggressive apology approach ("I'm so sorry you felt that way"). On its corporate blog in a post titled "Not So Silent Bob," a reference to Smith's famous role and now infamous Twitter outburst, the airline apologized and explained its actions.[12]

> Mr. Smith originally purchased two Southwest seats on a flight from Oakland to Burbank – as he's been known to do when traveling on Southwest. He decided to change his plans and board an earlier flight to Burbank, which technically means flying standby. As you may know, airlines are not able to clear standby passengers until all Customers are boarded. When the time came to board Mr. Smith, we had only a single seat available for him to occupy. We are responsible for the Safety and comfort of all Customers on the aircraft and therefore, we made a judgment call that Mr. Smith needed more than one seat to complete his flight.

The airline also took to Twitter. That's a best practice—to respond on the same social media platform where the crisis is taking place. The results were mixed, but at least Southwest was authentically engaged, even asking Smith to follow them so they could send him a direct message. (On Twitter, you can only direct message people who follow you.) Southwest tweeted:[13]

> @ThatKevinSmith hey Kevin! I'm so sorry for your experience tonight! Hopefully we can make things right, please follow so we may DM.

The airline, in 2010, had more than one million followers on Twitter. Many were unhappy to read about Smith's accusations. Southwest had to acknowledge that and it did through numerous tweets.

> Hey folks—trust me, I saw the tweets from @ThatKevinSmith I'll get all the details and handle accordingly! Thanks for your concern!
>   I read every single tweet that comes into this account, and take every tweet seriously. We'll handle @ThatKevinSmith issue asap.

The airline also offered him a $100 voucher to which Smith tweeted the following:

F*** your apologetic $100 voucher, @SouthwestAir.

Smith responded further by saying he often purchased two tickets on Southwest not because he was required to, but because the airline was cheap to fly and he valued the extra space. He tweeted the following after he boarded another flight.

Dear @SouthwestAir, I'm on another one of your planes, safely seated & buckled-in again waiting to be dragged off in front of the normies.
    And, hey? @SouthwestAir I didn't even need a seat belt extender to buckle up. Somehow that shit fit over my "safety concern"-creating gut.

By evening, Southwest finally found an appropriate "voice" on Twitter to navigate itself out of this self-inflicted crisis.

I've read the tweets all night from @Thatkevinsmith – he'll be getting a call at home from our Customer Relations VP tonight.
    @ThatKevinSmithAgain, I'm very sorry for the experience you had tonight. Please let me know if there is anything else I can do.

Smith wasn't done yet. He posted two-dozen video statements on YouTube about his Southwest experience. In one (http://www.youtube.com/watch?v=Y5UoTWAMQwU), he expressed no regrets about tweeting his experience especially, he says, if it saved other fat people from embarrassment.[14] Remember, the customer is always right and, in Smith's case, gets the last word.

Southwest's Mistake Chain. *Do not humiliate a passenger*! Do not humiliate *an overweight* passenger! Do not humiliate a *famous* passenger!
    This is such an important point we felt the need to say it three times. It is not good business practice and it is not good human practice

either. Customers do not like "mean girl" behavior by the companies they do business with, either directed at them or directed at others while they watch. It makes them uncomfortable which makes them seek out other businesses to do business with.

Those customers are also likely to be on the social media. If they witness something like humiliating a person who is overweight, they will likely tweet about it.

Never blame the victim. In its initial statement, Southwest Airlines put the onus on Smith and assumed that because he purchased two airline tickets he did so because of his weight. Smith denied that was his reasoning. Southwest looked petty by making that assumption and singled Smith out again for his weight.

Accusations of discrimination are serious matters. Nowhere in its blog post did Southwest denounce discrimination or say it takes any accusations of discrimination seriously. It should have. Staffs must be properly trained on how to enforce sensitive policies like the "customer of size" one. Judging by how Smith was treated, Southwest did not train its crews on the best ways to implement the policy.

Lessons Learned. Southwest Airlines issued a response, explained its policy, and reached out to Smith personally. But, Southwest will forever (thanks to Google and Smith's persistence on his weekly podcasts) be known as the airline that kicked "Silent Bob" off the plane for being too fat. Social media crises are a black mark on an organization or business forever. Kevin Smith understood the power of the social media and used it at the airline's expense.

Airlines, or any business, have to really think through policies that might target a specific kind of customer before implementing that policy. The "customer of size" policy in theory makes sense, but practically it is a hornet's nest to comply with.

That policy is a crisis waiting to happen again to Southwest or any other airline. The next passenger likely will not be famous but could easily use Smith's experience to build a discrimination lawsuit against the airline. One of the main functions of public relations is to protect the reputation of the company. That "bodyguard" mentality includes thinking through all policy decisions to make sure the company will not be vulnerable to accusations of discrimination and possible lawsuits.

Airlines should more clearly define the "customer of size" policy and have better procedures in place to implement it when necessary. We suggest an airline senior manager at the airport who can have that awkward but necessary conversation *before* that passenger boards the plane. The airline should also incorporate some compassion into how it executes the policy. No one likes to be told he or she is fat, much less in front of a large group of strangers.

Airlines should also think about transparency when it comes to informing passengers about the policy. Perhaps airlines could have passengers read the policy before they are allowed to book a ticket online. Or, perhaps airlines could post the policy at the airport check-in counters, much like the displays about carry-on luggage, so people are aware of it before they board their flights.

Service-based businesses that have social media accounts (and they should all have social media accounts) need to have people monitoring them all the time. Smith's tweets barely hit people's Twitter feeds before they were being retweeted and magnified very quickly among influencers online. It happens that quickly today. Unfortunately, for Southwest, it would have another high-profile altercation that would play out on Twitter a year later in 2011.

Finally, as an airline that prides itself on inclusion and diversity, Southwest got trapped into looking discriminatory. Organizations must walk the walk and talk the talk or, stated differently, do not talk east but walk west.

The Second Crisis

The next year, Southwest faced another crisis fueled by social media. It once again suggested the airline's claims on openness and diversity might not, in fact, be true.

Leisha Hailey is the openly gay actress best known for her role as "Alice" on "The L Word," the popular and provocative Showtime drama about a group of lesbians living in Los Angeles. Hailey is also the lead singer of the eletro-pop band, Uh Huh Her. In September 2011, she and girlfriend Camilla Grey boarded a Southwest Airlines flight in Baltimore, Maryland. The two, by Hailey's own admission, kissed. In a matter of minutes, Southwest found itself, yet again, in an instant social media crisis, this time battling accusations of homophobia.

The Crisis. Hailey and her girlfriend were in their seats and, according to Hailey, they exchanged a "small peck on the lips." A Southwest Airline flight attendant saw that peck much differently. According to Hailey, the flight attendant approached the couple, scolding them for their public display of affection and saying, "we needed to be aware that Southwest Airlines is a family oriented airline."[15] The couple, by their own admission, got into a verbal altercation with the crewmember that led to them being removed from the flight.

Hailey, like Kevin Smith a year earlier, unleashed a torrent of angry tweets aimed at Southwest. She also called for a boycott of the airline (see Figure 6.2).

At whiplash speed, Southwest Airlines found itself in the midst of another instant social media crisis, a particularly ugly one too with

Figure 6.2. Leisha Hailey's Tweets.

accusations of homophobia. With six loaded tweets punched out one after another, Hailey had social media's rapt attention. Her first tweet was re-tweeted over 2,500 times.

Once social media pays attention, traditional news organizations soon follow. Accusations of homophobia are always troubling, but when you are an airline that prides itself on its gay pride tolerance those accusations threaten to expose a hypocrisy that becomes almost impossible to fix.[16] In 2011, to make matters worse, Southwest was the official airline of GLAAD, the Gay & Lesbian Alliance Against Defamation.

Southwest's Response. Southwest Airlines responded quickly with a brief statement on its website (http://www.swamedia.com/releases/9063e4d3-dabc-4ab2-9016-fa4c19895894). That statement said, in part:[17]

> Initial reports indicate that we received several passenger complaints characterizing the behavior as excessive. Our crew, responsible for the comfort of all Customers on board, approached the passengers based solely on behavior and not gender.
>
> The conversation escalated to a level that was better resolved on the ground, as opposed to in flight. ... We are ready to work directly with the passengers involved to offer our heartfelt apologies for falling short of their expectation.

The statement, though, failed to define the excessive behavior. It also did not use the statement as an opportunity to remind stakeholders of its gay-friendly policies (and partnership with GLAAD). Unlike with Kevin Smith and the highly personal corporate blog post, Southwest did not address Hailey by her name but instead referred to her as a generic passenger.

Hailey and her girlfriend, in turn, responded with a press release of their own (http://www.msopr.com/press-releases/uh-huh-her-camila-grey-and-leisha-hailey-respond-to-southwest-airlines-incident/).[18] That release acknowledged they raised their voices but only in response to their treatment by the flight crew. It said, in part:

> We want to make it clear we were not making out or creating any kind of spectacle of ourselves. It was one, modest kiss.

Southwest then followed up with another press release that reaffirmed its version of events.[19] It still did not name Hailey but offered the passengers a full refund. It also did not directly address Hailey's accusations of what the flight attendant said to her. It left a lot of people on social media wondering, did the flight attendant use the phrase "family airline?" Southwest did, though, reaffirm its full support for the LGBT community.

> We do not tolerate discrimination of anyone for any reason.

It was a heartfelt response, but one that was 24 hours late. All of these comments were left out of its initial statement. Instead, the release looked like it was playing catch-up. Much like with Kevin Smith's altercation, Southwest Airlines' "luv" for its stakeholders unfortunately felt more like hate to some.

Southwest's Second Chain of Mistakes. The best defense is always a strong, multi-layered offense during a crisis, especially when accusations such as homophobia are being lobbied. Southwest, much like with the Kevin Smith altercation, initially defended its position without denouncing the charges of discrimination.

The airline failed to define what it considered "excessive behavior." It also came across as determined to "win" the argument against Hailey rather than negotiate a peaceful understanding. It turned the altercation into a "he said, she said" game of one-upmanship. Both sides are telling their perceptions of the truth.

Like its "customer of size" policy, Southwest must do a better job at training crews to exhibit more compassion as they enforce controversial policies.

Lessons Learned. Southwest spent years cultivating a relationship with the gay and lesbian community. It is during crises like this one Southwest should have been able to call upon those LGBT relationships to advocate for it, especially on the social media where GLAAD has a robust presence.

Do not assume that because a celebrity is not "A List" she has no influence. Hailey had a loyal following as an openly gay actress and singer. She was also an attractive and articulate person. She is going to get attention from news organizations. She got it on the social media.

Respond and then keep responding. One of the best tactics any company can employ during the initial social media crisis siege is to not adopt a siege mentality. The more a company can get on the social media and respond to tweets personally, the faster a crisis can be capped. Even if that response is just a "here's a link to our statement."

Also, *reach out to your critics directly*. Say you are sorry about the unfortunate experience, and you would like to talk about it. Or tweet out that you have reached out to the person. The key here is to demonstrate some action. Southwest puts a heart in its logo. It should have showed that heart in its responses.

Whether Leisha Hailey is gay or not is not the issue. The issue is how does an airline handle two passengers who are engaged in an excessive display of public affection? How does an airline define "excessive?" Remember also that attitudes and laws are changing in the United States toward gay couples. Airlines need to find a balancing act among the needs of all stakeholder groups.

American Versus Alec: A Losing Proposition?

Background

Actor Alec Baldwin holds the impressive record of most appearances as host of the perennial "Saturday Night Live." Ironically, an altercation involving Baldwin and American Airlines on December 6, 2011, had all the makings of a skit for the show. For its part, American Airlines had already been through a rough news week. Its parent company, AMR, filed for bankruptcy and media outlets were reporting on a lawsuit filed by a family claiming a bad meal served on an American Airlines flight caused the death of their loved one, a passenger on that flight. The last thing the airline needed was a fight with a celebrity on Twitter, especially with one as bombastic as Baldwin. But, that's exactly what they got.

The Crisis

After Baldwin boarded a flight in Los Angeles, he began playing the "Words with Friends" game, a Scrabble-like game, on his iPad. According to American Airlines, the crew asked the actor to shut off his electronic devices in preparation for takeoff. Baldwin refused and, according to the airline's flight crew, got up and went into the airplane's lavatory, disrupting the plane's departure from the gate. Because he refused to comply, he was removed from the flight.[20]

Baldwin immediately took to Twitter in a tirade against American Airlines and one of its flight attendants.

> Flight attendant on American reamed me out 4 playing WORDS W FRIENDS while we sat at the gate, not moving. #nowonderamericanairisbankrupt
> #theresalwaysunited.

After Baldwin boarded a later American Airlines flight, he continued tweeting.

> Now on 3 o'clock American flight. The flight attendants already look…smarter"
> Last flight w/American. Where retired Catholic school gym teachers from the 1950's find jobs as flight attendants.

By that evening, Baldwin, an avid tweeter, deleted his account. (As of December 2012, he is back on Twitter again with a new account handle.)

American's Response

We have included this case study because, unlike its competitors, American Airlines handled this incident fairly well. It had no choice.

Clearly, any time a personality engages in social media brand bashing, a business has to respond. Baldwin had millions of followers. The story became a trending topic, and media covered it. The airline had just filed bankruptcy and did not need another negative story about itself in the news.

American Airlines initially reached out to Baldwin on Twitter instead of issuing a statement.[21]

> @alecbaldwin Mr. Baldwin we are looking into this. Please DM (direct message) us contact information.
>
> Our flight attendants were following Federal safety procedures on electronic devices when aircraft door is closed.

But, because Baldwin would not let up on his social media tirade and it was getting traction, compelling the airline to issue a statement on its Facebook page the next day. It said, in part:[22]

> Since an extremely vocal customer has publicly identified himself as being removed from an American Airlines flight on Tuesday, Dec. 6, we have elected to provide the actual facts of the matter....When the door is closed for departure and the seat belt light is turned on, all cell phones and electronic devices must be turned off for taxi-out and takeoff...This passenger declined to turn off his cell phone when asked to do so at the appropriate time....The passenger ultimately stood up (with the seat belt light still on for departure) and took his phone into the plane's lavatory. He slammed the lavatory door so hard, the cockpit crew heard it and became alarmed, even with the cockpit door closed and locked.

The statement was spot on. Media reports backed up the airline's version of events as did other passengers on that flight. A passenger named Michael J. Wolf tweeted:[23]

> On an AA flight at LAX. Alec Baldwin removed from the plane. We had to go back to the gate. Terrible everyone had to wait

Champion boxer Oscar De La Hoya was also a passenger on that flight and confirmed Baldwin had gotten angry. It did not help Baldwin that he had a history of histrionics. Remember his YouTube tirade against his daughter that became so public (http://www.youtube.com/watch?v=lgj6NEk9xEw).[24]

Baldwin responded to the airline statement with a long bylined apology, which ran under the title "My Flying Lesson" in The Huffington Post Blog.[25] In it, he apologized to the other passengers, ate some crow, and took a few more shots at the stewardess. In an unsuccessful attempt to make light of the incident, he appeared in a skit on "Saturday Night Live" as the American Airlines captain.[26] But, by that point, people were laughing at him and not with him (http://www.nbc.com/saturday-night-live/video/weekend-update-capt-steve-rogers/1372901/).

Baldwin's Chain of Mistakes

In today's celebrity obsessed, 24-hour news cycle, businesses must respond if a public figure takes to the social media to tarnish its brand. But American Airlines commendably did not allow itself to get pulled into a "he said, she said" communication dynamic with Baldwin, despite his numerous attempts to bait the airline into doing so. Instead, the airline waited 24 hours before it told its side of the story to the public and media. As a result, Baldwin looked like a fruitcake on a tirade, not a reasonable, disgruntled passenger.

The airline's communication teams had created incredibly strong messaging of safety and security issues. They employed them in a solid, tight statement on its Facebook page.[27] At the same time, Baldwin and his publicity team misread how the public would react to his diva behavior. The comments about him we analyzed on the social media were overwhelmingly negative, with many people calling him words unfit for print here. In comparison, the sentiment toward American Airlines was positive.

Lessons Learned

Respond quickly, especially if a well-known person is attacking your business or organization on social media. The longer you let someone else define the parameters of the crisis, the harder it is to get in front of it. But sometimes, it is best to issue a statement and then wait it out. As Baldwin continued his tirade for a few more days, he looked more and more foolish.

Pay attention to the conversations online. American Airlines' team was able to assess fairly quickly that people were supportive of the airline's decision to remove Baldwin from the flight. One commenter posted on www.cbsnews.com:[28]

> Hoorah to AA for taking a stand! Please continue discouraging boorish behavior!

Finally, *in every crisis lies an opportunity.* We used the Chinese characters to stress this in the opening chapter—that a crisis can either be a moment of danger or a moment of opportunity. Zynga, who manufactured the "Words with Friends" game, jumped into the conversation on Twitter to promote the game.[29] It tweeted:

> Hey @AmericanAir, do not ground @AlecBaldwin for playing. A.B.S.U.R.D is worth at least 11 points in @WordsWFriends.

That could have proved a "dangerous" move by being perceived as taking advantage of a crisis situation. But, this crisis was ridiculous in nature and therefore Zynga played off the humor in that.

Airline Crisis—The Bottom Line

Three of the four crises we covered in this chapter involved well-known personalities who were regular social media users. A celebrity connection automatically brings heightened interest and more social media rubbernecking than usual.

Any business, organization, or entity on social media must regularly monitor for conversations about themselves or their competitors.

If your organization finds itself in the midst of a social media crisis, remember to listen closely to the conversations about the crisis via tweets, comments posted on Facebook, and comments posted in response to news articles online. Those conversations are your "finger on the pulse" of how the crisis is playing out among your stakeholder groups. Consider our case studies. People who supported the passengers of JetBlue and Kevin Smith, were mixed about the personal display of affection factor with Leisha Hailey and her girlfriend, and were fully behind American Airlines because of Alec Baldwin's obnoxious behavior.

Instant social media crises can feel hard to navigate because of their unpredictable path. But, the conversation online can help you make more informed decisions as you draft a strategy, develop messages, and work to take back control of the conversation.

Lou Says: It's not often that Forbes Magazine, a notorious critic of businesses, calls the American Airlines corporate communications effort a "masterpiece," but that's just what they did in this piece the next week (http://www.forbes.com/sites/erikamorphy/2011/12/11/companies -cant-win-the-twitter-wars-especially-against-the-likes-of-alec-baldwin/).[30]

However, there's a caution in their piece as well. Companies have to accept the fact people and news organizations LOVE celebrity-driven stories, and that, as Forbes says, "people are funnier than companies."

But, remember the love affair can be short-lived. So have patience. In the short-term, do what you need to do—quickly respond, be sincere, fix the crisis—and know that there will be little long-term fallout. People and media will move on to another celebrity in another instant social media crisis because, of course, there will always be one.

Susan Says: In August 2012, my sister called me from her cellphone as she and her family sat on the runway waiting out an indefinite flight delay for a trip to Aruba. She was irritated the flight attendant wouldn't give her extra milk for her young daughter. She knew I was Twitter savvy and wanted me "to put something on there" to let the airline know she was upset.

The call amused me given that Lou and I were working on this book at the time. My sister's reaction is not unlike millions of airline customers today who have low tolerance for bad airline service. She could have just as easily called the airline's 1-800 number to talk to customer service. Instead, she wanted to vent her displeasure via social media.

When I asked her about her protest choice, she told me she wanted as many people as possible to know about the airline's behavior. She, much like Kevin Smith, Leisha Hailey, and Alec Baldwin, viewed social media as an effective tool to publically shame airlines that do not deliver quality customer service. Social media have become *that*—an effective means to impose a "scarlet letter" on any business that doesn't deliver when it should.

That's why it's so important for companies to monitor social media, measure sentiment, and respond accordingly. They need to ask themselves "Is this conversation on social media merely noise or a tipping point for something more, like an impending crisis?" My sister's situation was "noise," while most of the cases we just examined were potential tipping points.

By the way, I didn't tweet on behalf of my sister. She had to hang up for takeoff.

CHAPTER 7

Racing from the Storm

Background

It is safe to say that New York City was not prepared for the arrival of Hurricane Sandy in late October 2012. The city, businesses, and individuals may have planned for the storm by purchasing batteries, filling their gas tanks, and evacuating their homes but no one could have foreseen just how much damage Hurricane Sandy would cause among communities along the Eastern coast. With at least 100 deaths, thousands of homes and businesses damaged or destroyed, and damage estimated in the billions, the devastation rattled even the toughest of New Yorkers who survived the September 11 attacks a decade earlier.

Super storm Sandy hit the Bahamas on Thursday, October 25, 2012, and began to migrate up the East Coast. New York City Mayor Michael Bloomberg held a press conference on October 25 in which he stated:[1]

> There will be a lot of rain along the whole East Coast, certainly in southern Florida, and then coming up. If this storm merges with another storm coming from the Ohio Valley, it has the potential to give you real weird weather, like snow, and a lot of rain and high winds. On the other hand, it might just go out to sea, and they just do not know. What we are doing is we are taking the kind of precautions you'd expect us to do, and I do not think anybody should panic.

New York City had itself a mother nature induced crisis and was responding accordingly. The Metropolitan Transportation Association shut down bridges, suspended subway, train, and bus schedules to encourage people to stay home, stay safe, and stay alive.

On Monday, October 29, 2012, Hurricane Sandy made landfall in the northeast region of the United States. The "super storm" beat expectations and wreaked havoc on much of New Jersey, New York City, and Long Island. Areas like Coney Island were under water. Fires destroyed entire neighborhoods in Queens. Parts of the iconic Seaside Heights, New Jersey, amusement park were pushed into the Atlantic Ocean, forever destroying many childhood memories. Most of the area was left paralyzed. Millions were without public transportation, power, electricity, or heat. It was an emotional, overwhelming crisis that prompted many people to retreat to social media for information and community during an angst-ridden time.

By Tuesday, the social and mainstream narrative was one of both shock and survival. The obvious subjects were raised.

- What communities were still in grave danger?
- How could people get in and out of NYC with subway lines, tunnels and airports flooded?
- When will electricity be restored?

The electric utilities, meantime, were struggling with a crisis of their own. No one could blame them for underestimating the strength of the storm—it was unprecedented and unpredictable. But they brought criticism on themselves because of their communications failures.

Nick Ashooh, a 15-year veteran of the industry, explains that the key is setting accurate expectations and communicating them effectively. The electric companies were consistently too optimistic about their recovery abilities and were sending customers without power to their website for updates. "You have to do whatever it takes to communicate," said Ashooh. "We resorted to leaflets when nothing else worked."[2]

The communication failures engendered frustration and anger among customers and public officials alike. Kathy DeFillippo, Deputy Mayor of Roxbury Township, New Jersey, summed it up. "Their communication was just rhetoric. We needed facts."[3]

The Long Island Power Authority (LIPA) faced the most criticism. In the end, its operations chief, vice president of customer service, and a trustee appointed by then-Governor Spitzer, all resigned, all insisting their departure had nothing to do with the crisis. Really?

Later in the week gas lines became violent as patience thinned and tempers flared. Police and first responders were inundated with rescues and the need to deter looting in areas of the city left in the dark.

Could New York City host the 2012 ING New York City Marathon just 6 days after the biggest storm to ever hit the east coast?

Decision Point

In the immediate wake of the storm, New York City's Mayor Bloomberg, Deputy Mayor Howard Wolfson, and New York Road Runners (NYRR) President Mary Wittenberg faced a massive, highly emotionally charged decision—should they cancel one of the greatest, most anticipated marathons in the world or leverage the race as a symbol of New York's strength and resilience in the face of adversity?

The situation was unprecedented in the race's history. Even after the attack on the World Trade Center on September 11, 2011, officials were still able to proceed with the race six weeks later.[4] The same was true after Tropical Storm Irene in 2011. The circumstances surrounding Hurricane Sandy created not only a crisis caused by the environment, but also a crisis that threatened to damage the bottom line of the race and cost the local economy precious dollars spent by the influx of more than 47,000 athletes and millions of spectators.[5]

The decision also carried potential long-term implications for the reputation of the race and local leaders, all of whom answer to different audiences. The NYRR president's primary audience is made up of amateur and professional runners from around the world and race sponsors, with New Yorkers serving only as a secondary audience. The mayor and deputy mayor answer to the people of New York.

Staying the Course

Initially, City Hall and the NYRR decided to continue the race and transform its purpose. Strategies of the committee responding to the situation included:

- leverage the race as a point of unity for the greater New York City community;

- use social media channels to inform athletes, spectators, media and residents, as well as support press conferences and interviews;
- position the race as an event to benefit and re-build the New York City area; and,
- ask runners to help boost awareness and generate visibility.

The marathon committee sent out messages from the race committee on Facebook, Twitter, and the race website. They re-named the event the "Race to Recovery"[6] and announced the creation of a foundation with proceeds going toward hurricane relief and recovery.[7] Their call to action asked the athletes to donate a minimum of $26.20 (the total mile count of the marathon), to the cause of Hurricane Sandy recovery.[8]

The Crisis Debate

It did not take long before anger among the New York residents erupted, and the race began to create a division—those supporting the decision to continue the race and those in favor of its cancellation or postponement. People whose homes were destroyed, who were still in the dark, and who faced unimaginable personal loss were outraged by the potential to distract resources and emergency responders from their needs.

And, there were plenty of visual reminders of the distraction the race was already causing. Trailers were lined up from 66th to 72nd streets on Central Park West. City workers were erecting tents. A food truck was set up in Central Park. And, generators were put in place. The influential blog, Gothamist, summed it up in its headline: "Food Trucks, Generators To The Rescue For... Sunday's Marathon?[9]

By Friday, less than 48 hours before the race was set to begin in Staten Island and one day after announcing the "Road to Recovery" Foundation, officials once again met to discuss next steps in response to the firestorm of messages on Facebook and other social media platforms from fans, residents of the city and others, as well as the barrage of news articles and heated "water cooler conversations" throughout the region.[10]

In addition to Twitter, the New York City Marathon Facebook page became a heated forum for debate over the 2012 race's fate.[11]

At least two Facebook pages emerged in response to the city's decision to continue with the marathon, including one named "Cancel the 2012 NYC Marathon."[12] On that page, people debated the issue and posted requests for volunteers. The highly engaged page manager posted rules for respectful posts, responded regularly, had lengthy conversations with visitors without hostile or confrontational language and posted public responses to inbox messages. One message from the page manager in response to an inbox message read:

> HI Marty, Thank you for your thoughts. I have thought about it. And you are right the city can use the money. I know this is not a simple issue and there are pros and cons to both but I am speaking from a perspective of logistics. It will be 5 days—not 5 weeks or 5 months from the day of this disaster. The city is struggling with so much.
>
> If a person was just in a car accident and was in the hospital with injuries they can't go to work no matter how much they may need the money, right? They would have to stay and recover, get stronger, heal a bit, then go back and work their butts off. I feel the city is still in the hospital. Give it time...[13]

Newspapers and television also prominently featured stories covering the increasingly divided opinions on the race's continuation. An article in the *New York Times* cited worries over stretched emergency resources.[14] The same article talked about Mayor Bloomberg's economic rationale behind continuing the race—a race that makes a multi-million dollar contribution to the local economy.

Retracing Their Steps

Bowing to public sentiment and pressure from every direction, city officials and marathon leaders held a late day press conference on Friday, November 2, 2012, announcing the historic decision to cancel the 2012 ING New York City Marathon.

The joint announcement acknowledged the mixed public opinions, both positive and negative, toward the initial decision to continue.[15]

They repeated their rationale for the initial decision to continue and gave their reasons for a new choice. They used social media messages and spokespersons to support the announcement and explain next steps for those affected by the late cancellation of the race.

The ING New York City Marathon Facebook page carried a message to support the press conference message:

> The City of New York and New York Road Runners announce that the 2012 ING NYC Marathon has been canceled. While holding the race would not require diverting resources from the recovery effort, it is clear that it has become the source of disagreement and division. We cannot allow a controversy over an athletic event—even one as meaningful as this—to distract attention from all the critically important work that is being done to help New York City recover from the storm. New York Road Runners will have additional information in the days ahead and we thank you for your dedication to the spirit of this race. We encourage runners who have already arrived in New York City to help with volunteer relief efforts.[16]

The cancellation message generated more than 1,000 comments and 3,000 likes by Facebook fans, who also shared it with their network of contacts more than 600 times.[17] The marathon committee made a limited number of comments to posts by fans of the page.

The Fallout

The crisis did not stop there. Facebook fans continued to comment with mixed emotion. Some who seemed to be athletes cursed the race for canceling after they had spent months training for the event. Others commented that they understood why the race needed to be canceled despite the disappointment they felt.[18] In the days after the intended date of the race of the marathon, the committee continued to post messages to update the marathon community as to its actions, to discuss options to make up for the missed race and to explain that it was working to make a difficult situation better. President Mary

Whittenberg also accepted interviews from a variety of national news outlets.

Analyzing the Communication

Corporate communication experts Doorley and Garcia say that leaders of corporations and organizations must always remember: "Reputations are won or lost in a crisis."[19] The actions and communications surrounding the 2012 Marathon offer a stunning example of that impact. The initial decision outraged media, politicians, citizens, and athletes alike. The final decision to cancel a few days later and several missteps in between failed to stem the outrage.

Officials certainly began acting quickly. As soon as it was clear that the storm was a threat, they began talking about strategy. Their Facebook posts talked about watching the progressing weather conditions. They made the decision early to re-focus the purpose and spirit of the event into something dedicated to hurricane relief, rather than individual causes. They recognized that this storm could disrupt business and seem to have gathered a team of people to make a decision on next steps. Posts to social media also began early on to let stakeholders know that the race committee was on top of a potential situation.

The initial decision was designed to express empathy toward the victims. Re-focusing the event's purpose and establishing a charitable foundation were designed to make the event meaningful to the storm victims. The announcement to cancel included a direct apology from both the Mayor and the race organizers, but their apology came across as defensive and insincere. The *Baltimore Sun* reported, "In cancelling the Marathon, NYC flunked the sincerity test."[20] Their apology was a classic, passive-aggressive response. Instead of apologizing for their insensitivity to the plight of New Yorkers, according to the *Sun*, they "blamed the growing controversy about holding the race as their reason for canceling it."[21] The controversy, they argued, distracted from the recovery. Ms. Wittenberg, in a letter to the race participants, took it one step further—blaming exaggerated media coverage for creating antagonism toward the event and its participants.[22] She continued to contend, even in the face of overwhelming evidence to the contrary, that the marathon would not have diverted resources away from the recovery.

Lessons Learned

The New York City Marathon crisis offers some of the most poignant lessons about the speed with which a crisis must be addressed, the need to be prepared, and the critical role of understanding and listening to your audience.

Race officials clearly should have had a plan in place, recognizing that unpredictable events in New York City (storms, strikes, terrorist attacks, and so forth) might disrupt the race and understanding that the decision to cancel or delay would be enormously difficult. Once the magnitude of the storm was understood, they could have implemented that plan. By doing so, they might have made a better initial decision and had communications in place to deal with it.

City and race officials, however, did not take into account all audience views/sentiments. The question of whether to continue or not was certainly a testable one. They needed to reach out to runners and residents alike, and/or their social media communities, to test sentiments around a potential cancellation. Communication needed to be managed more carefully as well. By neglecting to remove some pre-scheduled tweets about readying for the race, officials seemed to be out of touch.[23] They also needed to target their communication to insiders more effectively. They failed to inform registered amateur and professional athletes of their cancellation decision before the news conference began.[24] As a result, they lost the opportunities to have the insiders act as ambassadors for their decision.

Parting Comments

Lou Says: If the Mayor and the organizers had followed the simple guidelines of crisis management this situation might have been avoided or at least mitigated. There was no excuse for not having a plan in place. C'mon, this is the race that faced the challenges of Irene and 9-11. They failed to satisfy the reasonable expectations of the people involved, and that was the cause of their black eye.

Susan Says: #NYCMarathon was a trending topic on Twitter in the days following Hurricane Sandy. I actively participated in that social media conversation in part because of a very personal connection. I was born and raised on Staten Island, NY. I felt strongly the city should have cancelled the marathon with so many residents, particularly in Staten Island and Queens, suffering.

> **susan rucci** @susanrucci   2 Nov
> 20 dead now from Hurricane Sandy on #StatenIsland.
> #NYCMarathon still going forward. bitly.com/ShrM4W
> Expand

> **susan rucci** @susanrucci   2 Nov
> Heartbroken by #StatenIsland devastation. NYC always had weird
> relationship w SI but seriously CANCEL #NYCMarathon, help
> residents. #NOW
> Expand

That's the gift of social media during a crisis. It taps into real-time sentiment about an issue. There was a groundswell of support for cancelling the marathon on Twitter, Facebook, and in the comments section of online news articles. The data were there; it was up to NYC Mayor Bloomberg and his staff to pay attention to it. Finally, they did.

> **susan rucci** @susanrucci   2 Nov
> #NYCMarathon cancelled, per WNBC.
> Expand

CHAPTER 8

A Less Than "Progressive" Approach

Background

Progressive Insurance has been around for decades, but only captured the public's attention a few years ago when it launched a quirky, fun advertising campaign featuring Flo, the "perfect" employee, who has boundless energy and loves helping customers save money on their insurance policies. Those ads have catapulted the insurance company into the same ranks as rivals Allstate, State Farm, and Geico.

That's a long way from its beginnings in 1937 when Jack Green and Joe Lewis formed the insurance company in Mayfield Village, Ohio. Today, Progressive provides auto insurance for personal and commercial vehicles and professional liability insurance for businesses in 25 states.

The company helped cement its reputation as different from the others by providing its customers with comparable quotes from other insurance companies, so the customer can see how Progressive's quote stacks up against the competition. The company also pioneered the use of technology in insurance sales. It was also the first to offer online applications and approvals through its website.

But, it is really the ads featuring Flo that have attracted the attention and helped Progressive expand its customer base exponentially (see: http://youtu.be/itDejkU20Ig).[1] As shown in Figure 8.1, Flo's smiling face permeates all of Progressive's marketing materials including the company website, commercials, and is used as the avatar on many of its social media platforms. Business Insider said, "She consistently rates way above average in E-Poll's surveys of branded characters" which makes the quarter of a billion dollars a year spent on ads by Progressive worth the investment.[2]

Figure 8.1. Progressive's smiling spokesperson.

Progressive is now one of the largest insurers in the United States, with more than 10 million policies. It is a popular choice among younger drivers too because of its discounted rates.

Kaitlynn Fisher was one of those drivers.

The Accident

On Jun 19, 2010, while driving through a green light in Baltimore, Maryland, Fisher's Honda was *t*-boned by a Ford Explorer driven by Ronald Hope. Hope ran a red light causing the intersection collision. Twenty-four-year-old Kaitlynn died in the crash.

Hope was underinsured, but his insurance company settled with Fisher's estate. That settlement though was not enough to cover Fisher's substantial student loans she incurred as an engineer student at Johns Hopkins University. Loan companies often go after surviving family members for the outstanding debt. Fisher's Progressive policy included coverage for accidents with underinsured drivers. Her family assumed it would be the beneficiaries of her policies. They assumed wrong.

Over the next 2 years, Fisher's family fought Progressive to pay on her policy. The family claimed Progressive continuously low balled them with settlement offers well below what Kaitlynn's policy was written for. The family decided to sue Progressive. According to Maryland law, the Fisher family would first have to sue Ronald Hope, the driver who killed Kaitlynn. State law required the family to first establish in court Hope was negligent in order to force Progressive to pay the amount the Fishers believed they were owed.

On August 10, 2012, the jury found Hope responsible for the accident, thus establishing the legal precedent necessary to force Progressive to pay $760,000 and additional costs to the Fisher family. Although the decision was final by court, the case was not over just yet—and the social media were about to take this tragedy for the Fishers and turn it into a crisis for Progressive.

The Crisis

In early August, Kaitlynn's older brother, Matt, decided to harness the power of the social media to share the news of his family's fight for justice with Progressive. With just a handful of tweets and two blog posts on his Tumblr account Matt got everybody's attention, including national media (see Figure 8.2).[3]

On August 13, 2012, Matt's tweet linked to a post on his Tumblr account about his sister's death and his family's fight with Progressive. That tweet was re-tweeted 1,526 times. What caused that kind of reaction? Matt made a shocking accusation about Progressive (see Figure 8.3).[4] In that blog post, titled, "My Sister Paid Progressive Insurance to Defend Her Killer In Court," Matt accused Progressive of offering legal representation to the man who was responsible for her death.

> At the trial, the guy who killed my sister was defended by Progressive's legal team. If you are insured by Progressive, and they owe you money, they will defend your killer in court in order to not pay you your policy.

His post got nearly 12,200 re-blogs and notes.

Until this, Progressive had remained silent, citing legal and customer privacy concerns. On August 14, 2012, one day after his inflammatory

Figures 8.2 and 8.3. A brother's fight for justice.

post, Progressive released a statement on its website offering its condolences to the Fisher family and denying Matt's accusations.[5]

> To be very clear, Progressive did not serve as the attorney for the defendant in this case. He was defended by his insurance company, Nationwide.

Progressive kept its response brief and vague, only adding fuel to a social media firestorm. Take a look at just a handful of comments posted on the company's own website in response to the statement:[6]

> But were you on his side at all? Against the family of the deceased?
>
> Posted on 8/14/2012 at 2:18 PM by Nathan

> This is a very insulting statement. Good luck with your PR strategies..so fair they are a big failure.
>
> Posted on 8/14/2012 at 2:21 PM by ann

> What's not clear is Progressive's involvement with the case and what role your company played in the situation. Your PR department has failed to communicate that in a clear, concise, and responsible manner, which is much of the reason why your company is receiving the negative publicity we've seen over the past 24 hours.
>
> Posted on 8/14/2012 at 2:22 PM by Joey Beachum

> This doesn't make you seem any less heartless. In fact, I am now convinced of your callousness in this situation. Shame on you.

Matt immediately took to his Tumblr account a second time to refute Progressive's assertion it did not offer legal representation to the man responsible for his sister's death.[7]

> At the beginning of the trial an attorney identified himself Jeffrey R. Moffat and stated that he worked for Progressive Advanced Insurance Company...he then sat next to the defendant...he proposed the idea that the defendant should not be found negligent in the case.... I wrote about this case on my blog because I felt that, in the wake of my sister's death, Progressive had sought out ways to meet their strict legal obligation while still disrespecting my sister's memory and causing my family a world of hurt...their statement disavowing their role in the case, a case in which their attorney stood before my sister's jury and argued on behalf of her killer, is simply infuriating.

On August 16, 2012, Progressive released a second statement on its website announcing it had reached a settlement with the family and further clarifying its actions in the courtroom.[8]

Though there was considerable public interest in this case and we know many of you saw mentions of it on social media and news outlets, we also believed it was inappropriate to share further details while those discussions were ongoing. As of this morning, an agreement has been reached with the Fisher family to settle the claim...Under Maryland law, in order to receive the benefits of an underinsured driver claim, the other driver must be at fault. Sometimes this can be proven without the need for a trial, but in Ms. Fisher's case, there were credible conflicting eyewitness accounts as to who was at fault. A trial was necessary so that a jury could review all of the evidence and come to a decision. In those circumstances, under Maryland law, the insurance company providing the Underinsured Motorist coverage is considered a defendant. As a defendant in this case, Progressive participated in the trial procedures on our own behalf while Nationwide represented the other driver.

Progressive, through a veil of legalese language, admitted it was *in fact* in the courtroom. In that second statement, Progressive also announced it had reached a settlement with the Fisher family.

The Chain of Mistakes

Progressive should have known it would never win the public relations battle over Kaitlynn Fisher's tragic death once Matt Fisher took his sister's story to the social media. The insurance company should have settled immediately, no matter the cost.

Progressive found itself in the midst of a social media crisis yet it remained silent during the critical early days when emotions were running high. The company let Matt define Progressive through a series of highly inflammatory tweets and Tumblr blog posts that painted a chilling portrait of an insurance giant using unfathomable tactics to avoid their legal obligation to the Fisher family.

The company's responses were tepid at best. It seemed Progressive wanted to hide and act like nothing had happened. As a result, the company ended up making matters much worse. The company focused too much on legal principles and totally forgot about its reputation and its customers.

When the company did reply on its official Twitter page, the comments sounded insensitive and robotic. Progressive's response— saying the same phrase over and over and linking to previous statements on the company website—simply infuriated people. Their vague and indirect statements included "fulfilling our contractual obligations" and "we also believed it was inappropriate to share further details while those discussions were ongoing." Their statement that "... Progressive did not serve as the attorney for the defendant in this case. He was defended by his insurance company, Nationwide"[9] sounded like a partial truth, especially when compared to the brother's comments.

The responses on the various social media, including on the company's own social media pages, were overwhelmingly negative. It needed to do more than just announce it reached a settlement with the family. It needed to explain its actions and reassure customers. Figure 8.4 contains some of those reactions.

Speed is critical in social media communication, but it is equally important in an organization's behavior. Progressive needed to sort out the details in this case and get it resolved with the family much more quickly. Progressive's behavior seemed to contradict its own vision and values. On Progressive's website the company shares its vision and core values:[10]

To reduce the human trauma and economic costs associated with automobile accidents. We do this by providing our customers with services designed to help them get their lives back in order again as quickly as possible. Governing out vision, decisions and behavior are our core values—pragmatic statements of what works best for us in the real world. These core values include: integrity, Golden Rule, objectives, excellence, and profit.

The company's behavior and communication with the Fisher family did not appear to dovetail with those core values.

Figure 8.4. Reactions on social media.

Lessons Learned

While hiding behind the legal technicalities, the company lost credibility and took a serious hit to its reputation. People, especially social media users, want to hear genuine responses from companies. Instead, Progressive offered robotic, insensitive statements which gave social media users the control in the conversation that was taking place.

Throughout the crisis, Progressive showed little to no compassion for the Fisher family. The company never apologized for upsetting the family and dragging out the process. Progressive stated several times it offered its "deepest sympathies" to the Fisher family, but the statement felt contrived and bit passive aggressive too.

Progressive should have assessed the situation, developed an action plan, and communicated it broadly. Instead, it used language that seemed driven by litigation fears. Instead of worrying about legal, Progressive should have worried about its reputation.

The Progressive brand took a major hit as a result. Flo no longer seemed like a fun, happy brand ambassador but a caricature of a slick insurance salesperson. This self-inflicted crisis that played out so publicly on the social media and attracted such an eclectic mix of media (from CBS News to the Glenn Beck radio show) damaged the company's reputation and cost the insurance giant a lot more than the $750,000 settlement.

Parting Comments

Lou says: I worked at Aetna for 10 years. There were 120 lawyers in the law department. So I know how a company can be terrorized by legal threats. This case proves that in spades. The language Progressive used could only have come from a lawyer. No other human species would talk in such circumspect terms. By making a distinction where there was no difference in the public's eyes, the company sounded like Bill Clinton, parsing words in the Monica Lewinsky case ("...it depends on what the meaning of is, is"). If it walks like a duck and quacks like a duck, it is a duck. No matter what legal distinction might be made about the role of Progressive's lawyers in the courtroom, it sure looked like they were arguing against their client.

Susan says: I actually learned about this story via the social media. I saw hashtags for #katiefisher and #progressive, clicked on them, and found myself down the social media rabbit hole following this instant social media. This is the type of story news organizations love to cover. Matt Fisher was very "TV friendly," a term used when I worked in broadcast news to describe someone who was attractive, well-spoken, and appealing. Having come from journalism, I knew how this story would play out: a beautiful young woman whose life was tragically cut short, a grieving family seeking justice, and an evil insurance company that will not do the right thing. I have seen this movie before. The bad guys lose.

CHAPTER 9

"Refrigerator Gate" in China

In September 2011, Luo Yonghao, a popular blogger in China complained on his blog about a Siemens refrigerator that he had bought 3 years before. He said that the refrigerator's door was difficult to close.

Siemens' response began a social media crisis that haunts the company to this day.

Background

Siemens, the German multinational electronics giant, employs nearly 400,000 people in almost 200 countries. The company has operated in China for 140 years and now manages a network of more than 60 regional offices there.[1] Siemens makes electronics-related products, from power generation systems to light bulbs and everything in between. The company website lists three core values—*responsibility, excellence,* and *innovation.*[2] The company markets and services home appliances in China, including refrigerators, through a joint venture with the Chinese company, Boxi.

Globally, Siemens maintains an extensive presence on the social media, with accounts on all the leading services. In addition to Facebook, Twitter, and YouTube, the company participates in regional and local social media as well. In China, it has an official page on the country's most popular social media network, Weibo.[3]

Luo Yonghao, the protagonist in this crisis, started his blog "Bullog" in 2006 and in just a few years it has grown to one of the most popular and widely read by the Chinese.[4] Because of that, China's communist government shut the site down in 2007 but that did not stop Luo. "Bullog" reappeared online with an international version in 2008. The 40-year-old former English teacher and high school dropout quickly became an Internet celebrity because of his liberal views and edgy tone.

He has three million regular followers, and has become a popular after dinner speaker in China.[5]

The Rise of the Social Media in China

The rise of the social media in China has fundamentally changed the relationship between brands and their consumers, and put new demands on those brands for responsive customer service. According to the China Internet Network Information Center (CNNIC), the number of the Chinese Internet users (all Chinese citizens aged six or above that accessed the Internet over the past six months) reached 384 million in 2009, an increase from 2008 of 22.6 % to 28.9% from 2008 to 2009. In metropolitan cities such as Beijing and Shanghai, the Internet penetration rate was over 45%.[6]

Online social media are a major part of the Chinese Internet culture since the first online discussion forum that was launched in 1994. Since then, netizens—a netizen is a person actively involved in online communities—use forums, discussion groups, blogs, micro-blogs, and social networking sites to express themselves, share information, and exchange ideas. According to Michael & Zhou, more than 80% of Chinese Internet users today get their news and information from online sources, including social media. Now, only 67% of Internet users say that they read newspapers, compared with 79% in 2007.[7]

Weibo, the Chinese equivalent to Twitter, in particular, has become a major information source for Chinese public opinion. Each Weibo post has a 140-character limit. The big difference though is the amount of information that can be delivered via 140 Chinese characters is usually four to five times what can be communicated with 140 English characters. The ability to insert photos, outside links, and video on Weibo further adds to Weibo's influence among the Chinese. Weibo users actively post and repost news, which makes each user akin to an independent media outlet. It is widely said in China that "When one's Weibo has more than 100,000 followers, its influence is equal to that of a big city daily; if the number reaches 1 million, it's comparable to a national newspaper; once the number goes beyond 10 million, it's the equivalent of a TV station; and if the number soars to 100 million, it's equal to the China Central Television."[8]

Take Sina Weibo as an example, an equivalent micro-blogging tool of Twitter, which was launched in August 2009 by the biggest Web portal in China, Sina Corporation (NASDAQ: SINA).[9] According to the company's 2011 annual report, Weibo has more than 50 million active users per day, and 10 million newly registered users per month (Sina, 2011); its subscribers reached 250 million by November 2011; over 75 million messages were forwarded or circulated daily (China Daily, 2011).[10]

According to the Blue Book issued by the Chinese Academy of Social Sciences' Journalism and Communication Research Institute, "Network media in China is growing from the grass-roots to the mainstream of the country's distribution of news."[11]

The Crisis

September 29, 2011

Luo Yonghao posted a complaint on his micro-blog complaining about his refrigerator door, and about Seimens' tepid response to his problem.[12] His blog post was reposted more than 3,000 times. In two months, nearly 500 netizens left messages to Luo, echoing his complaint and telling him that their Siemens refrigerators had the same problem. "In the beginning, I thought that the problem was an isolated case," said Luo. "However, after thousands of netizens echoed my complaints, I was sure that this was a design flaw in some batches in a series of Siemens refrigerators."[13]

October 15, 2011

Siemens issued a statement on its official micro-blog. The company said that it had noticed netizens' complaints about the door of its refrigerators. Their statement said,

> Some consumers encountered the problem of uneasy closing of the refrigerator door, and the company has been in contact with them.

At the same time, the company contacted Luo directly through its public relations firm, which asked Luo what he needed from Siemens. Luo recorded the conversation and posted it on his micro-blog.[14] The firm promised to grant Luo's request, which asked Siemens to (1) acknowledge the quality problem; (2) publicize the serial numbers of the problematic refrigerators, and (3) set up an agenda to fix the problem. However, if Siemens failed to deliver on this commitment, Luo threatened to smash Siemens refrigerators in front of the company's Chinese headquarters in Beijing.

November 20, 2011

Siemens issued a tepid statement in response to Luo's request, which failed to satisfy him. As more and more consumers complained to him about the doors on their Siemens refrigerators, Luo continued to say that certain models of the Siemens refrigerators had design flaws.

To protest against the German company's vague and reluctant response to his issues, Luo staged an event where he smashed three Siemens refrigerators in front of the Siemens Chinese headquarters in Beijing. Those three refrigerators belonged to Luo himself, famous Chinese musician, Zuo, and Chinese writer, Feng. The smashing protest was all recorded on video too (to see this, go to: http://www.youtube.com/watch?v=bAW2LPRn0vQ).[15]

Luo Yonghao takes a sledge hammer to the problem.

In response, Siemens released a statement on its official micro-blog, suggesting Luo should have taken rational and legal actions to protect his rights.[16] In the statement, the company emphasized that Boxi, one of its Chinese joint ventures, was responsible for the production, sale, and after-sale services of the Siemens refrigerators sold on the Chinese market. It "encouraged" Boxi to investigate and solve the problem.

The response of the social media to Siemens' statement was fast and loud. Consumers pointed out that the refrigerators were labeled with the Siemens brand and buyers were encouraged to contact the "Siemens hotline" with questions or problems. Other commentators also noted that when it comes to selling fridges, the company was happy to label them as "Siemens refrigerators," but when problems emerged they mysteriously changed into "BSH fridges."

November 21, 2011

Another famous blogger and several journalists claimed that the public relations firm hired by Siemens met with major traditional media, and warned that Siemens would not advertise on any media that published the news about Luo smashing Siemens refrigerators in front of its head-quarters.[17] Still, almost every portal website and major media outlet covered the incident the next day.

Ongoing Activities

While this crisis was brewing, Boxi/Siemens held several media conferences in Beijing, Shanghai, and Guangzhou on other topics. When asked about quality problems, Boxi's vice-president responded, "Why should we acknowledge that it was our mistake when we actually made no mistakes?"[18] He said the Siemens refrigerators met every standard, and suggested that the consumers were actually closing the doors the wrong way. He blamed the door problems on the consumers not the company.

December 4, 2011

Because the Chinese traditional media continued reporting on the refrigerator doors, the President and CEO of Siemens Home Appliances in China stepped forward in a video to defend the brand.[19] He said only a small number of Siemens refrigerators were affected. Generally speaking, he asserted, Siemens refrigerators did not have quality problems. Still, he apologized to those who were not satisfied and assured customers that the company would solve the problem by (1) setting up a Weibo account to respond to complaints; (2) provide free on-site inspection; and (3) add a door closer device when it was technically possible.

Luo responded to the CEO video with another round of questions, including (1) which refrigerators were affected, (2) under what condition would Siemens add door closer devices, and (3) how would Siemens help those who were unable to connect to Weibo to solve the problem?[20] However, Siemens failed to answer any of the questions.

December 20, 2011

Luo was fed up. He invited media, hundreds of netizens and consumers to a famous theater in Beijing. He gave a one-hour lecture on the whole issue and smashed another ten Siemens refrigerators.[21] Luo also announced that he would be creating a documentary film about Siemens refrigerators and launching an advertising campaign to inform the public about the quality problems with Siemens refrigerators. War had been declared.

The Ongoing Problem for Siemens

Luo continued to put up thousands of posts for more than a year, containing pictures, videos, and outside links about Siemens, mostly negative, on his micro-blog. Luo's micro-blog has now become a platform where consumers complain about all their Siemens products. Netizens even dubbed Luo with the unofficial title of "Customer Service Supervisor of Siemens."[22] They began turning to Luo asking him for help dealing with their concerns about Siemens products.

The crisis has taken a bite out of Siemens' market share. A Chinese research company indicated that the market share of Siemens refrigerators has been shrinking since September, 2011.[23]

Siemens Mistake Chair and Lessons Learned

Siemens made several critical mistakes in responding to its refrigerator crisis. Among them the following were the most critical.

- *Failure to respond to a seemingly minor problem*—The origin of the Siemens crisis was a blog post on Sina Weibo. It seemed to be a minor problem—a consumer's complaint posted on his own blog. It can be inferred from Siemens' response that the company must have thought that it could deal with the issue without too much publicity. It released a statement through the same vehicle—Sina Weibo—insisting that its refrigerators did not have a quality problem.

Luo has more than 2.1 million followers. He is considered an opinion leader and role model in China. After Luo's first blog, Siemens should have paid attention to those numbers and recognized Luo's influence among its stakeholders. Moreover, as more and more consumers emerged complaining the same problem, the company should have seen the trend unfolding.

Lesson 1: All Complaints Are Not Created Equal

- *Talking east and walking west*—Poor judgment accelerated Siemens' mistake chain and fueled the crisis.

Publicly, Siemens insisted that its refrigerators did not have a quality problem. Then, the company had its public relations firm contact Luo "confidentially" to try to get him to stop complaining. Privately, (or so it thought) it promised to acknowledge the quality problem, publicize the serial numbers of the faulty refrigerators and set an agenda to fix the problem.

Additionally, Siemens tried to "kill" the story in traditional media. It threatened to pull its advertising from any publication that ran the story of the refrigerator smashing.

Lesson 2: Effective Communication Is Always Grounded in Transparency and Authenticity. Not Bullying and Threats

- *Parsing words* –The company's first response was an attempt to shift the blame to Boxi—its "independent" joint venture—while the refrigerators carried the Siemens brand.

In a crisis, compartmentalizing the problem does not work. Siemens mistakenly assumed that the public would see a distinction where there is no difference in their eyes. Siemens should have accepted responsibility and taken steps to get the problems resolved.

Lesson 3: Take Responsibility, and Talk Straight

Parting Comments

Lou Says: The global communications team at Siemens is highly respected in PR circles. Somehow, though, its staff in China failed to live up to that PR reputation. It shows how tough the job of the global CCO can be. Monitoring 24/7 worldwide, aligning company communication worldwide, and ensuring the same level of quality everywhere is a daunting task. Just look at the lengths PR Giant Golin Harris has gone to with its new digital monitoring network, "The Bridge" (to see the lengths taken by Golin Harris go to: http://golinharris.com/#!/approach/the-bridge/)[24]

Susan Says: Instant (and, in the Siemens' case, long-lasting!) social media crises aren't just threats to the U.S.-based businesses today. Populations, particularly in emerging markets like BRIC (Brazil, Russia, India and China) are embracing social media networks too.

This is an important case study for a few reasons. Most businesses are multinational now and serve a global consumer base. Management of those businesses must monitor social media from a global perspective. It shouldn't assume a social media fueled crisis in China or Brazil would go unnoticed by stakeholders in other countries, particularly in the United States. Apple came under fire after U.S. media reported its Chinese Manufacturing partner, FoxConn Technology, engaged in deplorable labor practices that reportedly led to numerous worker suicides. The Apple-FoxConn story attracted a lot of U.S. media coverage, including a very thorough investigative piece in *The New York Times*.[25]

But, even though the U.S. media covered the story, the social media in the United States was mostly silent on the issue.

Huffington Post contributor Adam Hanft called the silence "selective empathy."[26]

But, Apple and other global businesses shouldn't get too comfortable with that "selective empathy" apathy. After all, we are all global citizens today. There will be that tipping point when bad corporate behavior, no matter where it's taking place, will become intolerable even among the most "selective" customers too.

CHAPTER 10

Herding Cats—The Challenge of Controlling Employees

Watch these two YouTube videos: (http://www.youtube.com/watch?v=PKUDTPbDhnA) and (http://youtu.be/1D9PikBzNNo). You will see social media crises unfold in a matter of seconds for shipping giant FedEx and pizza delivery king Domino's.[1] What you will see dumbfounded social media users:

- A FedEx package that is supposed to be delivered with care is instead carelessly tossed onto a customer's property.
- Two Domino's employees videotaped themselves disgustingly violating sanitary and health codes as they prepare food at a Domino's store in North Carolina.

Usually, it is a management decision that causes a company's self-inflicted social media crisis. But, we are now going to examine two instant social media crises created by company employees instead. These are important case studies because they underscore how disgruntled or bored employees can create an instant social media crisis for a company.

Employees are a key stakeholder group for any business, but especially in service-based industries where they are often the first impression made with customers. These videos were watched thousands of times in a matter of a few days. Domino's clearly had the tougher crisis of the two to navigate. After all, it is easy to dismiss the FedEx employee as disgruntled. But, the Domino's video taps into most people's fear of restaurant employees spitting in their food. Its crisis also took place in 2009 when companies were still trying to understand how much influence social media had among people. It turns out it had a lot of influence.

YouTube had already been changing the social media landscape since its creation in 2005. Its tagline, "Broadcast Yourself," encouraged anyone to post anything from videos of cute kittens to countless parodies and imitations of singer Beyonce's "Single Ladies (Put A Ring On It)."

In this chapter, we look at how FedEx and Domino's Pizza successfully navigated these crises, proving social media crises, like any crisis, can be tamed by utilizing smart crisis management skills.

FedEx

Background

FedEx, the global courier delivery service, is headquartered in Memphis, Tennessee. Founded in 1971, the company has expanded over the decades since to a global presence with a workforce of 290,000 employees, according to its website.[2] Holidays, particularly Christmas, are big money makers but also taxing as the workforce struggles to get incredibly large volumes of packages shipped on time to locations around the world. According to FedEx, December 12, 2011, was its busiest day in the company's history. On that day, it doubled its average daily volume, moving an estimated 17 million packages through its system as holiday shoppers rushed to purchase last minute online gifts.[3]

One of its most famous advertising campaigns made the promise "When It Absolutely, Positively has to be there Overnight." Unfortunately, that promise was not exactly kept on December 19, 2011.

The Crisis

Like countless others, a Miami customer made an online purchase during the last quarter of 2011. His Samsung computer monitor was due to arrive at his home on December 19. The customer made sure he was home for the arrival of this package and even kept an eye out for the FedEx courier. FedEx did deliver the package, not by ringing the customer's doorbell but rather by tossing the fragile box over the gate and walking away. The customer caught the delivery on his home security camera.

This customer, who we will now call by his YouTube screen name, "Goobie55," uploaded a 21-second video of a FedEx Express van pulling up to his home, the courier exiting the van holding a Samsung computer monitor box, walking up to Goobie55's gate and tossing the box over it. The FedEx guy then returned to his van with no regard for the box or its fragile contents.[4] As may have seen earlier in this chapter if you went to YouTube, the FedEx logo of the van and the courier's uniform are clearly visible. He is a FedEx employee. Watch it again to see how those 21 seconds created an instant social media crisis for FedEx (http://www.youtube.com/watch?v=PKUDTPbDhnA).

Once Goobie55 posted the video to YouTube, the customer service crisis quickly became a public relations crisis one too. Within 48 hours, the video had over two million views.[5] It became a viral hit—to FedEx's dismay.

The Company's Response

FedEx did not ignore Goobie55's YouTube video. It reacted quickly. Within 48 hours, FedEx posted a response on its blog[6] and released its own video response on YouTube.[7] Matthew Thornton III, FedEx Senior VP OF Express U.S. Operations, looked directly into the camera and delivered a sincere, authentic, and apologetic message.

It was a perfect response for a number of reasons. First, Thornton apologized, said FedEx personally reached out to the affected customer, and reassured all stakeholders from customers to employees to investors that FedEx was a reliable, professional delivery service business. Second, he reiterated the company's customer service slogan: "To make every FedEx experience outstanding." Third, Thornton also turned a negative-Goobie55's damaging video into a positive by announcing FedEx would begin using it for future training to ensure that unfortunate customer experience would never happen again.

Even Thorton's own appearance enhanced the believability of FedEx's response. He was dressed in a suit and tie and spoke authoritatively in a well-lit, professional setting with a FedEx logo as the background. The visuals all said confidence, competency, and a company that was owning its mistake without shame. Thornton also stressed that the actions of one employee did not reflect the work ethic of the FedEx workforce. That was smart to do. By reinforcing this as an isolated incident, Thornton reassured all stakeholders, including employees, that FedEx saw this as out of line with the company's usual internal and external behaviors. And, *he defended FedEx without sounding defensive.*

Unfortunately for FedEx, despite their excellent response the video was just too juicy to die. It has become one of the most popular on YouTube, with nearly nine million views as of this writing, and growing (see Figure 10.1).

Figure 10.1. A screen shot from the YouTube video.

Lessons Learned

FedEx handled this crisis quickly and effectively. It said it was sorry, it reached out to the affected customer, and it reassured all stakeholders FedEx was a professional, reliable courier delivery business. That said, FedEx's crisis management cannot undo what was done. Thornton's apology was viewed less than 500,000 times on YouTube while Goobie55's video remains viral well after the incident was resolved.[8]

Despite the broad reach of the video, it seems now to be merely an entertaining diddy and not a real crisis for the company. Today, FedEx generates over $40 billion in revenue every year.[9] Fortune Magazine lists it as one of the Top Brands, as well as one of the best companies to work for too.[10] FedEx earns itself another title with us: *Best Practice in how to handle an employee created crisis on YouTube.*

Domino's Pizza

Background

In the 50 years since its creation, Domino's has made a lot of pizza deliveries. It is the second largest pizza chain in the United States (Pizza Hut is number one). According to its own website, Domino's delivers on average one million pizzas every day around the world.[11] Its busiest day? Super Bowl Sunday where the company works overtime to feed hungry football fans.

Today, the company has 10,000 global stores, a combination of company-owned and franchise owned. Five thousand of the stores are based outside the United States. It is known primarily for its pizza, but offers other entrees too. Domino's delivers, making it popular among college age students. It offers dependable food at reasonable prices. But, if you watch the video (http://youtu.be/1D9PikBzNNo), you can see that the company's dependability took a credibility hit when two employees are seen engaging in disgusting behavior in the kitchen.

Their account and videos are now gone. It was at http://youtube.com/whiteair2 !

0:12 / 1:11

A screen shot from the employee's video.

The Crisis

"In about 5 minutes it'll be sent out on delivery where somebody will be eating these, yes, eating them, and little did they know that cheese was in his nose and that there was some lethal gas that ended up on their salami. Now that's how we roll at Domino's," employee Kristy

Hammonds narrated as her work colleague, Michael Setzer, engaged in stomach turning behavior with food being used to make food orders.[12] Watch it again (just in case the first time wasn't nauseating enough for you http://youtu.be/1D9PikBzNNo).

Hammonds uploaded the video most likely on Sunday, April 11, or Monday, April 12, 2009, to YouTube. By Tuesday, the video caught the attention of bloggers who alerted www.GoodAsYou.org and www.consumerist.com, the non-profit subsidiary of *Consumer Reports*, which both posted the video on their websites.[13] From there, amazingly enough, two Internet "sleuths" were able to identify the store based off of the YouTube name, "Whiteair2," used by Hammonds as well as analysis of the video itself.[14]

By Tuesday night, the storeowner and corporate headquarters were both alerted. But, in that 24-hour period, thousands of people had already watched the offending video. By the time Hammond and Setzer were identified and fired, the video had over one million views on YouTube.

The Company's Response

On Wednesday, April 14, Domino's responded. It posted a statement on its website, created a Twitter account (http://www.dominosbiz.com/Biz-Public-EN/Extras/Cares/) and released a video on YouTube with a personal message from Patrick Doyle, President of Domino's USA (http://youtu.be/dem6eA7-A2I).[15]

Domino's President, Patrick Doyle, making an effective apology.

Doyle's response was textbook for best practice in crisis management. He did all of the following:

- Thanked the online community for its help.
- Called it an isolated incident but one the company took incredibly seriously.
- Said the two employees were fired and felony warrants were issued for them.
- Said the store where the incident took place was shut down and sanitized from "top to bottom."
- Said Domino's would re-examine its hiring practices.
- Reaffirmed Domino's commitment to providing high-quality food.
- Got personal. He said the incident "sickened" him knowing actions of two people impacted the global workforce of 125,000.

But, that response came 48 h after the offending video had gone viral.

Spokesperson Tim McIntyre told the *New York Times* on April 15, 2009, "We got blindsided by two idiots with a video camera and an awful idea. Even people who've been with us as loyal customers for 10, 15, 20 years are second-guessing their relationship with Domino's, and that's not fair."[16]

It may have not been fair, but it was true. A number of research outlets conducted polls in the aftermath of the crisis found that second-guessing was happening among customers. One online research firm confirmed Domino's reputation had taken a major hit among customers.[17] Another conducted a poll and found 65% of respondents who would previously visit or order Domino's Pizza were less likely to do so after viewing the offensive video.[18]

As for the guilty employees, one of them, Hammonds, pulled the video off YouTube and attempted her own crisis communication to save her job. According to Domino's, she emailed the company,[19]

"It was fake and I wish that everyone knew that!!! I AM SOO SORRY!"

Domino's did not accept her apology.

Lessons Learned

These kinds of crises are now a legitimate reputational threat in the age of social media. Any company is vulnerable, especially food service businesses. There is always someone now with a smartphone camera ready to capture and create an instant social media crisis for your organization. Two videos come to mind immediately: the 2007 rat infestation video at the KFC/Taco Bell in NY (you can find it at http://youtu.be/qvLDFtaL5HI)[20] or the one posted on YouTube of the guy taking a bath in the kitchen sink at a Burger King restaurant (http://youtu.be/rRFwcN_EOSU).[21] Both do more than make you lose your appetite. Postings like these can make a business lose its reputation.

Taco Bell, New York City.

The Key Is Preparation

Having clear policies in place on employee behavior, proper training and strong third-party relationships all help with the company's defense when an employee steps out of line.

Domino's should have done more to assure stakeholders all its franchises have the highest safety and health standards in place. Doyle should have gone into detail about the steps the company takes to ensure all franchises live up to corporate expectations of clean work environments. If they had quality standards established, they should have communicated them. If not, then they were in trouble from the outset.

As for the two guilty employees, we think it is safe to assume they were caught off guard by the instant social media crisis they created as well. In addition to their legal problems, they will be haunted by their stupid behavior forever online. Employers routinely Google prospective applicants' names when they apply for jobs. When you Google Kristy Hammonds and Michael Setzer, their names pop up connected to the Domino's crisis.

Parting Comments

Lou says: We were called in when a Denny's employee in Washington, D.C., refused service to two black Secret Service agents. The problem was Denny's didn't have any of the tools it needed to defend itself. They hadn't published standards of service for managers. They had no training in place or policies on discrimination. And they didn't have relationships with leading organizations in the African-American community. As a result, it took years to recover from the mistake of a single employee.

Susan says: These two crises, not surprisingly, got a lot of traction among traditional news media outlets, especially broadcast ones. If there is a crisis involving your company and visuals (either video or photos exist) you can bet media will cover it, particularly broadcast media because the crisis can be told very visually. That is why corporations need to respond within hours of an inflammatory video.

As a journalist, I was always baffled when companies would issue a "no comment" during a crisis. Talk! Reputable news organizations will always report both sides of a story. If all you say is "no comment," that's what will be reported. A "no comment" will not make a story go away. If anything, it creates more buzz. But, if you comment, especially with a video response, it will be inserted into the news report. Most news stories get at most 2 min in a broadcast. By giving a video response, you are taking time away from the damaging video being shown more in the report.

CHAPTER 11

Crisis Planning in the Conversation Age
(with Bernice Stevens)

In 2011, Burson Marsteller, a leading public relations firm, did a study on crisis preparedness in the age of social media.[1] More than 40% of business decision-makers reported it is harder to plan for a crisis today. Why? The rise of the social media has increased companies' vulnerability to crises, reported 55% of respondents. More than 80% saw that vulnerability gaining not losing traction too. Social media is a permanent fixture in society. Now, deal with it.

As we have discussed in our case studies, the social media can influence crises in a number of ways. It can cause them, react to them, or be some combination of the two.

Business Decisions

It would be great if every business decision a company made resulted in a win-win for all audiences. But often times business performance pressures force financially motivated decisions which are great for investors, but inevitably not so great for other stakeholder constituencies such as customers or employees.

Think of a layoff at corporate headquarters in a small city. When one of your authors was at Aetna, the company laid off 6,000 people in Hartford, Connecticut. The local papers featured the anguish of employees and concerns about the economic impact on the city. But the stock price went up. Fewer employees meant lower costs, which meant higher profits.

Social media now dramatically amplify issues that create tensions between companies and their customers. The crisis Netflix faced over the changes they made to their plans and prices serve as an excellent example (Chapter 3). Netflix made a business decision that was unpopular with its customers when it separated its DVD and streaming video plans and announced a new, more expensive price structure.

That happened on July 12, 2011. You would think the Netflix team would have been prepared for and anticipated some negative reactions from the marketplace. What customer willingly wants to pay more for a service? *That's just crisis planning 101.*

Yet, what Netflix was NOT prepared for was the speed and pervasiveness of the response on social media. When it posted the news on the corporate blog (http://blog.netflix.com/2010/11/new-plan-for-watching-instantly-plus.html) there were more than 11,000 comments in the first 48 hours. That grew to over 1.6 million comments within two weeks. "Cancel Netflix" sites popped up overnight (https://www. facebook.com/Cancel.Netflix?ref=ts&fref=ts). Competitors, like Blockbuster, responded immediately with enticing offers to disgruntled Netflix customers. Hey, *we never said social media crises are bad for everyone. What's a danger for you is an opportunity for me.*

Netflix defended its decision to the business community, predicting that most customers would stay because "each of our plans is an incredible value."[2] The marketplace did not agree. Netflix lost 800,000 customers by the end of September 2011. The company's stock tumbled from $289 a share on July 13th to $69 per share on November 3, 2011.

Self-Inflicted Harm

Large organizations, with thousands of employees on social media, cannot control everything that is posted. Duh! The Internet abounds with tales of rogue employees who leaked confidential information or spoke personally in an offensive way on company channels.

Like the Google engineer, who thought he was only posting to his personal friends, but who instead released a tirade on Google+ about the flaws in Google+ on the very day the service was launched.[3] (He somehow kept his job. He apparently activated a very good personal crisis communication plan.) Or the Tweet, on @ChrslerAutos, sent by an employee of their social media agency complaining about the drivers in Detroit, complete with an expletive.[4] (He was fired.)

And then there's Anthony Weiner—the married Congressman who posted photos of himself in his underwear (Chapter 4). That is bad enough. But, add in the chain of denials and subsequent expanding revelations. All of it collectively proved to be too much. (He resigned.)

Companies, too, can shoot themselves in the foot on the social media. Nestle, no stranger to crisis management, learned first-hand about the power of social media when it faced protests over its palm oil production's impact on the rainforests from Greenpeace.[5] People began posting altered logos of Nestle Products and Nestle responded with a post on its Facebook page threatening to delete any posts using an "altered version of our logos" (see Figure 11.1)

Figure 11.1. An example of the "altered" Nestle logos.

The response was immediate and pervasive. Protests over the intrusion of the company on free speech and expression flooded the social media. Within hours, the company issued a retraction and an apology. Nestle learned you might own the brand, but you do not own the conversation on social media. You should, though, participate.

Rumors and Hoaxes

High-profile brands are susceptible to all kinds of social media mischief. MacDonald's faced rumors its hamburgers contained worm meat. Other stories included the claim their stores charged a premium to

African-American customers because of the high incidence of robberies.[6] Then there's the rumor that turns out to be true—like Anthony Weiner's shorts!!

Social Media and Planning

In Chapter 1 we asserted that "the realities of people's reasonable expectations and the basic rules guiding crisis behavior and communication have not changed" despite the influence of the social media.

That holds true for crisis *planning* as well.

You still need the basic bases covered for crisis preparedness, namely:

- *Analysis*—of vulnerabilities that might affect you, their probability and potential magnitude, and the stakeholders affected by them.
- *Action Plans*—your goals, strategies, tactics, resources, and logistical needs in case a crisis hits.
- *Communication plans*—the structure for your communications plan, including goals, strategies, audiences, channels, messages, and tactical alternatives.

Be Like a Boy Scout—Prepare

So, what is different when you factor in the influence of the social media?

Begin by Accepting the Reality That It Can Happen to You

Bad things happen, even to good people and good businesses. Anticipate the worst. Be a skeptic. A customer service problem, a misbehaving employee, an event outside your control can all lead to a crisis. Assume it *will* happen not that it *will not*. You will never say, "I'm so sorry I spent all that time drafting a social media crisis plan that I never got to use."

Audit for Vulnerabilities

Identify the key areas where a crisis might occur and analyze each. A SWOT analysis (Strengths, Weaknesses, Opportunities, and Threats) can be a useful tool for the analysis of vulnerabilities.

Envision Potential Scenarios

Thinking ahead will help predetermine responses to different situations—"if this happens, we do that." It helps to simulate these scenarios in real time to test your responses as well as to train and test your people. Some people do not do well in crisis. It is better to find this out in simulation than during a real catastrophe. Run through the same real time exercise for social media. For example, a tweet goes out by a famous singer bashing your company, how do you respond? What do you say? We suggest do some reporting, track the conversation on Twitter, and then respond. All of this by the way should be happening within minutes, not hours and definitely not days.

Establish Crisis Protocols

Several crisis protocols need to be created: What is a crisis, who gets called (and how they can be reached at all times), who is in charge, who is at the table, who can speak for the company, who needs to be informed? How will information be disseminated, by whom, and how can privileged documents be protected?

Empower Your Team

The speed of the social media requires fast response. Delay is your enemy. With solid scenario planning and message development you should be able to empower your team to act on your behalf without delays caused by long approval processes or long waits gaining access to senior management. If the boss is in Los Angeles, and a crisis breaks in London, you cannot wait for her to wake up.

Identify the Resources the Crisis Team Needs

Should any equipment or supplies be kept on hand? What materials/ resources/ access does the communication team need? Where will budget come from as expenses are incurred?

Define Your Key Publics

In her book *Crisis Communications: A Casebook Approach*, Kathleen Fearn-Banks puts publics into four broad categories:[7]

> *Enabling publics*—those people with the power and authority to make decisions: the board of directors, shareholders, investors, and key executives. Notifying enabling publics is a priority.
>
> *Functional publics*—the people who actually make the organization work: employees, unions, suppliers, vendors, consumers, and volunteers in the case of nonprofit organizations.
>
> *Normative publics*—those people who share values with the organization in crises: trade associations, professional organizations, and competitors.
>
> *Diffused publics*—those people linked indirectly to the organization in crisis: the media, community groups, and neighbors of the physical plant.

Start Listening

All kinds of social media listening software can be found with the click of your mouse. Try socialbrite.org's webite for instance (http://www.socialbrite.org/2011/01/11/guide-to-free-social-media-monitoring-tools/)[8]

Social media fuel crises, but they also act like the canary in the coal mine. Decide who listens, for what, and when. Get 24/7 coverage. Bad things often happen on nights and weekends. Remember the lengths a leading public relations firm, Golin Harris, has gone to in order to monitor on behalf of their clients (Chapter 10). Their "Bridge" offers clients 24/7 news and social media monitoring through a global network of what they call "Holistic Engagement Centers."

Develop a Thorough Context for The Issues That Might Hurt You

What is your point of view? How has it manifested itself in practice? What protocols exist for hiring, training, and prevention? What philanthropy are you engaged in? Who can vouch for your practices? Do you engage third parties in performance evaluation? Knowing the answers to these questions and filling in gaps in performance ahead of time help define a broader context for issues that affect the company. Having this work done before a crisis hits saves time during a crisis.

Line Up Your Allies

Who will vouch for you? Who can attest to your character? Who from the affected community will speak kind words? These can be very powerful tools for mitigating damage. Explore how you work with third-party organizations. What joint programs are in place?

Inventory Your Reputation Assets

Have you received any awards? Each of these things helps frame a broader perspective of you during a crisis, but only if you have the documentation when you need it.

Finally, Document Everything

Records of the crisis plan, contact directories with emergency numbers, and all documentation must be accessible any time and any place. And documentation provides the basis for continuous improvement. Save the emails, save the posts. Take screen grabs of social media encounters if necessary. Record the timing and sequence of events. Procter & Gamble calls it "key learnings." Every crisis adds to your body of knowledge for dealing with the next one. And, there will be a next one. Count on it.

Conclusion

Respect the power of social media, especially in a crisis situation. Used effectively, the social media provides direct access to audiences—a one-to-many communications tool that opens up a dialogue with your stakeholders.

The social media can also make matters much worse. Social media creates opportunities for individuals and groups to oppose or criticize your organization. It magnifies those voices, be they an unhappy blogger in China (Chapter 10), an openly gay actress angry with her treatment by an airline crew (Chapter 6), or supporters unhappy with a non-partisan organization that makes a partisan decision (Chapter 2).

There are now large, energized communities on the social media listening and telling others what they heard whether by retweeting or "sharing" a post. News media is more and more influenced by those retweets and shares too.

Advance Preparation and Involvement in Social Media Is Key

Choose the platforms that best fit your organizations and get in the conversation. And put plans in place so that *when*, not *if* social media comes into play in a crisis situation you're prepared.

Crisis management is never easy. Social media might make it seem impossible. But a combination of sweat, brains, and heart will help your organization do its best to manage this essentially unmanageable environment.

In the end, follow Spike Lee's advice—"*Do The Right Thing*," and ultimately you will have navigated yourself an #epicwin not an #epicfail.

Notes

Chapter 1

1. Qualman, Eric (2012), New York, John Wiley & Sons. *Socialnomics*.
2. http://www.investopedia.com/#axzz2Np8QUcR1
3. http://www.comscore.com/Insights/Presentations_and_Whitepapers/2011/it_is_a_social_world_top_10_need-to-knows_about_social_networking
4. http://pewinternet.org/Reports/2011/Social-Networking-Sites.aspx
5. Scott (2010), p. 47.
6. Doorley and Garcia (2011).
7. Doorley and Garcia (2011), p. 117.
8. Groundswell (2008), p. 9.
9. http://www.indeed.com/q-Social-Media-jobs.html
10. Fink, Stephen (1989), New York, AMACOM.
11. Adubato, Steve (2008), New Brunswick, NJ, Rutgers University Press.
12. Doorley and Garcia (2011), p. 118.
13. Lecture material on crisis communication and management. University of Miami School of Communication, Coral Gables, FL.
14. Kubler-Ross, Elisabeth (2004), Berkeley, CA, Celestial Arts. On Life After Death.
15. Doorley and Garcia (2011), p. 312
16. http://digitalinfluencegroup.com/under/experience-the-social-shift-in-marketing-with-us/
17. Doorley & Garcia (2011), p. 116.
18. http://www.youtube.com/watch?v=7r4e5Wg4PDI Tiger Woods http://www.youtube.com/watch?v=Xs8nseNP4s0Exxon
19. http://www.youtube.com/watch?v=L0z5k0mc5yk
20. http://www.youtube.com/watch?v=j4XT-l-_3y0

Chapter 2

1. http://ww5.komen.org/AboutUs/AboutUs.html
2. http://www.washingtonpost.com/lifestyle/style/nancy-brinker-the-steely-force-in-the-susan-g-komen-foundation/2012/02/10/gIQAYjCfER_story.html
3. http://content.usatoday.com/communities/onpolitics/post/2010/08/karen-handel-concedes-in-close-ga-governors-race/1#.UUD18KX3CL0

4. http://www.huffingtonpost.com/2012/01/31/komen-for-the-cure-halts-_n_1245320.html

5. http://www.nytimes.com/2012/02/04/health/policy/komen-breast-cancer-group-reverses-decision-that-cut-off-planned-parenthood.html?pagewanted=all

6. http://www.huffingtonpost.com/2012/01/31/komen-for-the-cure-halts-_n_1245320.html

7. http://www.youtube.com/watch?v=Zb2vkbK66RY

8. http://www.youtube.com/watch?v=Hiz5EtNxtc8 http://www.nytimes.com/2012/02/04/health/policy/komen-breast-cancer-group-reverses-decision-that-cut-off-planned-parenthood.html?pagewanted=all

9. http://www.cbsnews.com/8301-201_162-57489685/komen-founder-to-step-down-as-chief-executive/

10. http://www.nytimes.com/2012/11/09/giving/komen-foundation-works-to-regain-support-after-planned-parenthood-controversy.html?pagewanted=all

Chapter 3

1. http://blog.netflix.com/2011/07/netflix-introduces-new-plans-and.html

2. http://blog.netflix.com/2011/09/explanation-and-some-reflections.html

3. http://youtu.be/c8Tn8n5CIPk

4. https://twitter.com/Qwikster

5. http://youtu.be/c8Tn8n5CIPk

6. http://money.cnn.com/2007/09/17/news/newsmakers/Ken_Chenault.fortune/index.htm

7. Doorley, John and Garcia, Helio Fred, 2007, New York, Routledge, Reputation Management.

8. Doorley and Garcia (2007).

9. Doorley and Garcia (2007).

10. Associated Press, October 24, 2011, http://finance.yahoo.com/news/Netflix-stock-plunges-on-apf-198318757.html

11. http://www.vanityfair.com/business/2012/02/netflix-201202

12. http://socialtimes.com/files/2010/11/FortuneNetflixReedHastings.jpg

13. http://www.nbc.com/saturday-night-live/video/netflix-apology/1359563/

Chapter 4

1. http://blog.twitter.com/2010/02/measuring -tweets.html

2. http://wwwmediabistro.com/alltwitter/twitter-active-total-users_b17655

3. https://twitter.com/BarackObama

4. Doorley, John and Garcia, Helio Fred, 2007, New York, Routledge Chapter 12. Reputation Management.

5. http://www.nytimes.com/2011/06/07/nyregion/timeline-of-weiner-case.html

6. http://www.thedailyshow.com/watch/wed-june-8-2011/the-wangover; http://www.thedailyshow.com/watch/mon-june-13-2011/the-wangover-part-ii

7. http://mashable.com/2011/12/14/ashton-kutcher-foot-in-mouth-award-tweet/

8. http://mashable.com/2012/12/12hurricane-sandy-google-search/

9. http://www.tmz.com/about

10. Orwell, George,1950, Penguin Group (USA) Incorporated, 1984.

11. http://www.huffingtonpost.com/2012/03/28/spike-lee-zimmerman-address-trayvon-martin_n_1385071.html

12. http://latimesblogs.latimes.com/gossip/2012/01/cher-twitter-hoax-kim-kardashian.html

13. http://www.washingtonpost.com/politics/rick-perrys-gop-debate-oops/2011/11/09/gIQAumzo6M_video.html

Chapter 5

1. http://www.reuters.com/article/2011/09/29/us-bankofamerica-debit-idUST RE78S4GQ20110929

2. http://www.whitehouse.gov/economy/middle-class/dodd-frank-wall-street-reform

3. http://thehill.com/blogs/on-the-money/banking-financial-institutions/97871-durbin-wins-battle-to-pass-qinterchange-feeq-legislation

4. http://money.cnn.com/2011/09/29/pf/bank_of_america_debit_fee/index.htm

5. https://www.facebook.com/groups/295542063792908/?ref=ts&fref=ts

6. http://www.huffingtonpost.com/2011/09/30/bank-of-america-debit-card-fees_n_989397.html

7. http://www.change.org/petitions/tell-bank-of-america-no-5-debit-card-fees

8. http://abcnews.go.com/Politics/video/bank-america-customer-protests-fee-14685050

9. http://video.cnbc.com/gallery/?video=3000049613

10. http://www.reuters.com/article/2011/09/29/us-bankofamerica-debit-idUST RE78S4GQ20110929

11. http://newsroom.bankofamerica.com/press-release/consumer-banking/bank-america-will-not-implement-debit-usage-fee

12. http://newsroom.bankofamerica.com/press-release/consumer-banking/bank-america-will-not-implement-debit-usage-fee

13. http://www.facebook.com/Nov.Fifth

14. http://www.charlotteobserver.com/2012/09/02/3497277/banking-anger-in-charlotte.html

15. http://www.charlotteobserver.com/2012/09/02/3497277/banking-anger-in -charlotte.html
16. http://www.bostonglobe.com/business/2011/12/25/interview-with-bank -america-ceo-brian-moynihan/8FTV3jGMojNgGqPmqvSKyO/story.html

Chapter 6

1. http://www.transtats.bts.gov
2. http://investor.jetblue.com/phoenix.zhtml?c=131045&p=irol-newsArticle &ID=1482885
3. http://www.jetblue.com/flying-on-jetblue/customer-protection/
4. http://youtu.be/-r_PIg7EAUw
5. http://www.kndo.com/story/15907998/jetblue-passengers-stuck-on-plane -for-7-hours
6. http://www.bloomberg.com/news/2011-10-30/-confluence-of-events-led-to -plane-s-stranding-on-tarmac-jetblue-says.html
7. http://money.cnn.com/magazines/fortune/most-admired/2012/snapshots/ 2068.html
8. See, for example: http://www.southwest.com/html/customer-service/extra -seat/index-pol.html; http://www.alaskaair.com/content/travel-info/policies/ seating-customers-of-size.aspx; http://www.united.com/web/en-US/content/ travel/specialneeds/customersize/default.aspx
9. https://twitter.com/ThatKevinSmith; http://mashable.com/2010/02/14/ southwest-kevin-smith/
10. http://twitpic.com/1340gw
11. http://abcnews.go.com/WN/kevin-smith-fat-fly/story?id=9837268
12. http://www.blogsouthwest.com/blog/not-so-silent-bob
13. http://mashable.com/2010/02/14/southwest-kevin-smith/
14. http://www.youtube.com/watch?v=Y5UoTWAMQwU
15. http://www.msopr.com/press-releases/uh-huh-her-camila-grey-and-leisha -hailey-respond-to-southwest-airlines-incident/
16. http://www.southwest.com/html/southwest-difference/community-involvement/ glbt/index.html
17. http://www.swamedia.com/releases/9063e4d3-dabc-4ab2-9016-fa4c19895894
18. http://www.msopr.com/press-releases/uh-huh-her-camila-grey-and-leisha -hailey-respond-to-southwest-airlines-incident/
19. http://www.swamedia.com/releases/9b8360a2-d68a-4012-b511-0a9579b24b7d
20. http://www.washingtonpost.com/blogs/dr-gridlock/post/alec-baldwin-removed -from-american-airlines-flight/2011/12/07/gIQAiaKYcO_blog.html
21. http://abcnews.go.com/blogs/entertainment/2011/12/alec-baldwin-what -happened-on-american-airlines-flight/

22. http://travel.usatoday.com/flights/post/2011/12/american-issues-statement
-on-alec-baldwin-incident/580193/1; https://twitter.com/search?q=%
23letalecplay&src=typd

23. http://gawker.com/5865677/why-was-alec-baldwin-just-kicked-off-his-flight

24. http://www.youtube.com/watch?v=lgj6NEk9xEw

25. http://www.huffingtonpost.com/alec-baldwin/american-airlines-service-_b
_1135201.html

26. http://www.nbc.com/saturday-night-live/video/weekend-update-capt-steve
-rogers/1372901/

27. http://www.cbsnews.com/8301-501465_162-57338656-501465/american
-airlines-releases-statement-on-alec-baldwins-accusations/

28. http://www.cbsnews.com/8301-501465_162-57338656-501465/american
-airlines-releases-statement-on-alec-baldwins-accusations/#postComments

29. http://www.businessinsider.com/let-alec-play-zyngas-response-to-baldwins
-tussle-with-american-airlines-2011-12

30. http://www.forbes.com/sites/erikamorphy/2011/12/11/companies-cant-win
-the-twitter-wars-especially-against-the-likes-of-alec-baldwin/

Chapter 7

1. http://thelede.blogs.nytimes.com/2012/10/25/hurricane-sandy-threatens
-northeast-and-mid-atlantic/

2. Personal conversation with Nicholas Ashooth, January 10 (2013).

3. Personal conversation with Kathy DeFillippo. January 10 (2013).

4. Burfoot, *Runner's World* (2012).

5. New York Road Runners, *Website* (2012).

6. McGoldrick, *Runner's World* (2012).

7. Burfoot, *Runner's World* (2012).

8. Belson, *Wall Street Journal* (2012).

9. http://gothamist.com/2012/11/01/food_trucks_generators_set_up_for_s.php
#photo-1

10. Burfoot, *Runner's World* (2012).

11. https://www.facebook.com/ingnycm?ref=ts&fref=ts

12. http://www.facebook.com/LetsGetNYCBackonHerFeet?ref=ts&fref=ts

13. Cancel the 2012 NYC Marathon, Facebook, November 2, 2012

14. http://www.nytimes.com/2012/11/03/sports/backlash-builds-as-new-york
-city-marathon-divides-city.html?pagewanted=all

15. http://www.nyrr.org/newsroom/nyrr-news-service/2012-ing-new-york-city
-marathon-cancelled

16. ING New York City Marathon, *Facebook* (2012).

17. ING New York City Marathon, *Facebook* (2012).

18. ING New York City Marathon, *Facebook* (2012).

19. Doorley & Garcia, *Reputation Management* (2011), p. 305.

20. http://articles.baltimoresun.com/2012-11-06/news/bs-ed-marathon-20121106
    _1_nyc-marathon-mayor-bloomberg-runners

21. http://articles.baltimoresun.com/2012-11-06/news/bs-ed-marathon-20121106
    _1_nyc-marathon-mayor-bloomberg-runners

22. http://gothamist.com/2012/11/03/nyrr_blames_marathon_cancellation_o.php

23. ING New York City Marathon, *Facebook* (2012).

24. Gambaccini, *Runner's World*, November 2 (2012).

Chapter 8

1. http://youtu.be/itDejkU20Ig

2. http://www.businessinsider.com/heres-the-evidence-that-progressive-is-about
   -to-kill-off-flo-2012-8

3. http://www.nytimes.com/2012/08/18/your-money/progressives-side-of-the
   -insurance-case-that-blew-up-on-the-internet.html?pagewanted=all

4. http://mattfisher.tumblr.com/post/29338478278/my-sister-paid-progressive
   -insurance-to-defend-her

5. http://www.progressive.com/understanding-insurance/entries/2012/8/14/
   statement_on_fisher.aspx

6. http://www.progressive.com/understanding-insurance/entries/2012/8/14/
   statement_on_fisher.aspx

7. http://mattfisher.tumblr.com/post/29432884849/today-in-response-to-my
   -blog-post-entitled-my

8. http://www.progressive.com/understanding-insurance/entries/2012/08/
   Default.aspx

9. http://www.progressive.com/understanding-insurance/entries/2012/8/14/
   statement_on_fisher.aspx

10. http://www.progressive.com/progressive-insurance/core-values.aspx

Chapter 9

1. http://www.siemens.com/about/en/worldwide.htm

2. http://www.siemens.com/about/en/values-vision-strategy/values.htm

3. http://www.weibo.com

4. http://www.newschinamag.com/magazine/top-blogger-profile-luo-yonghao/

5. http://www.newschinamag.com/magazine/top-blogger-profile-luo-yonghao/

6. http://www1.cnnic.cn/IDR/ReportDownloads/201209/t20120928_36586
   .htm

7. Michael & Zhou, 2010
8. http://www.china.org.cn/china/2011-12/08/content_24101840.htm
9. http://corp.sina.com.cn/eng/sina_intr_eng.htm
10. http://www.chinadaily.com.cn/bizchina/2013-02/21/content_16243933.htm
11. Xinhuanet, 2010
12. http://www.weibo.com/laoluoyonghao
13. http://www.weibo.com/laoluoyonghao
14. http://www.weibo.com/laoluoyonghao
15. http://www.youtube.com/watch?v=bAW2LPRn0vQ
16. http://www.chinahush.com/2011/11/20/china-internet-celebrity-luo-yonghao-smashes-refrigerators-at-siemens-beijing-headquarters/
17. http://www.eeo.com.cn/ens/2011/1124/216405.shtml
18. http://www.holmesreport.com/featurestories-info/12971/The-Top-12-Crises-Of-2012-Part-2.aspx
19. http://www.holmesreport.com/featurestories-info/12971/The-Top-12-Crises-Of-2012-Part-2.aspx
20. http://www.wantchinatimes.com/news-subclass-cnt.aspx?id=20111206000092&cid=1103
21. http://www.holmesreport.com/featurestories-info/12971/The-Top-12-Crises-Of-2012-Part-2.aspx
22. http://www.chinadaily.com.cn/china/2011-12/21/content_14300990.htm
23. http://chinadailymail.com/2013/01/04/chinas-top-ten-protesters-listed-by-tencent-news/
24. http://www.isnare.com/?aid=616947&ca=Computers+and+Technology
25. http://golinharris.com/#!/approach/the-bridge/
26. http://www.nytimes.com/2012/01/26/business/ieconomy-apples-ipad-and-the-human-costs-for-workers-in-china.html?pagewanted=all
27. http://www.huffingtonpost.com/adam-hanft/apple-foxconn-china_b_1392339.html

Chapter 10

1. http://www.youtube.com/watch?v=PKUDTPbDhnA for FedEx and http://youtu.be/1D9PikBzNNo for Domino's Pizza.
2. http://about.van.fedex.com/fedex-opco-history
3. http://news.van.fedex.com/package-volumes-projected-spike-december-12-fedex-hits-its-busiest-day-history
4. http://www.youtube.com/watch?v=PKUDTPbDhnA
5. http://blog.zap2it.com/pop2it/2011/12/fedex-shocked-after-seeing-video-of-package-throwing-employee.html
6. http://blog.van.fedex.com/absolutely-positively-unacceptable

7. http://youtu.be/4ESU_PcqI38
8. http://www.youtube.com/watch?v=PKUDTPbDhnA
9. http://fedexannualreport2012.hwaxis.com
10. http://www.fedex.com/in/enews/2013/february/fortune.html
11. http://www.dominosbiz.com/Biz-Public-EN/Site+Content/Secondary/About +Dominos/Fun+Facts/
12. http://youtu.be/1D9PikBzNNo
13. http://consumerist.com/2009/04/13/dominos-rogue-employees-do-disgusting -things-to-the-food-put-it-on-youtube/
14. http://consumerist.com/2009/04/14/consumerist-sleuths-track-down-offending -dominos-store/
15. http://www.dominosbiz.com/Biz-Public-EN/Extras/Cares/ and http://youtu.be/ dem6eA7-A2I
16. http://www.nytimes.com/2009/04/16/business/media/16dominos.html
17. http://research.yougov.com
18. http://www.hcdi.net
19. http://www.nytimes.com/2009/04/16/business/media/16dominos.html
20. http://youtu.be/qvLDFtaL5HI
21. http://youtu.be/rRFwcN_EOSU

Chapter 11

1. http://www.burson-marsteller.com/Innovation_and_insights/Thought _Leadership/Lists/SlideShares/DispForm.aspx?ID=27
2. http://blog.netflix.com/2011/07/netflix-introduces-new-plans-and.html
3. http://mashable.com/2011/10/12/google-engineer-rant-google-plus/
4. http://soshable.com/a-lesson-from-chrysler-tweet-with-ing-care/
5. http://www.prweek.com/uk/news/991636/NestlE-faces-Facebook-crisis -Greenpeace-rainforest-allegations/
6. http://www.cbsnews.com/2100-502303_162-20071227.html
7. Fern-Banks, 2012.
8. http://www.socialbrite.org/2011/01/11/guide-to-free-social-media-monitoring -tools/

References

Adubato, S. (2008). *What were they thinking? Crisis communication-the good, the bad and the totally clueless.* New Brunswick, NJ: Rutgers University Press.

Associated Press. (2011, October 24). http://finance.yahoo.com/news/Netflix -stock-plunges-on-apf-198318757.html

Bernoff, J., & Li, C. (2008). *Groundswell* (p. 8). Boston, MA: Harvard Business Review Press.

Burfoot, A. (2012, November 13) *In Praise of the NYRR and Mary Wittenberg* Runner's World (http://www.runnersworld.com/races/praise-nyrr-and-mary -wittenberg) Cancel the 2012 NYC Marathon, Facebook, November 2, 2012.

Doorley, J., & Garcia, H. F. (2007). *Reputation management.* New York: Routledge.

Fink, S. (2000). *Crisis management planning for the inevitable.* New York: AMACON.

Gambaccini, *Runner's World.* (2012, November 2).

http://digitalinfluencegroup.com/under/experience-the-social-shift-in-marketing -with-us/

http://mashable.com/2011/10/12/google-engineer-rant-google-plus/

http://soshable.com/a-lesson-from-chrysler-tweet-with-ing-care/

http://abcnews.go.com/blogs/entertainment/2011/12/alec-baldwin-what-happened -on-american-airlines-flight/

http://abcnews.go.com/Politics/video/bank-america-customer-protests-fee-14685050

http://abcnews.go.com/WN/kevin-smith-fat-fly/story?id=9837268

http://about.van.fedex.com/fedex-opco-history

http://articles.baltimoresun.com/2012-11-06/news/bs-ed-marathon-20121106_1 _nyc-marathon-mayor-bloomberg-runners

http://articles.baltimoresun.com/2012-11-06/news/bs-ed-marathon-20121106_1 _nyc-marathon-mayor-bloomberg-runners

http://blog.netflix.com/2011/07/netflix-introduces-new-plans-and.html

http://blog.netflix.com/2011/09/explanation-and-some-reflections.html

http://blog.twitter.com/2010/02/measuring -tweets.html

http://blog.van.fedex.com/absolutely-positively-unacceptable

http://blog.zap2it.com/pop2it/2011/12/fedex-shocked-after-seeing-video-of-package -throwing-employee.html

http://chinadailymail.com/2013/01/04/chinas-top-ten-protesters-listed-by-tencent -news/

http://consumerist.com/2009/04/13/dominos-rogue-employees-do-disgusting
-things-to-the-food-put-it-on-youtube/

http://consumerist.com/2009/04/14/consumerist-sleuths-track-down-offending
-dominos-store/

http://content.usatoday.com/communities/onpolitics/post/2010/08/karen-handel
-concedes-in-close-ga-governors-race/1#.UUD18KX3CL0

http://corp.sina.com.cn/eng/sina_intr_eng.htm

http://fedexannualreport2012.hwaxis.com

http://gawker.com/5865677/why-was-alec-baldwin-just-kicked-off-his-flight

http://golinharris.com/#!/approach/the-bridge/

http://gothamist.com/2012/11/01/food_trucks_generators_set_up_for_s.php
#photo-1

http://gothamist.com/2012/11/03/nyrr_blames_marathon_cancellation_o.php

http://investor.jetblue.com/phoenix.zhtml?c=131045&p=irol-newsArticle&ID
=1482885

http://latimesblogs.latimes.com/gossip/2012/01/cher-twitter-hoax-kim-kardashian
.html

http://mashable.com/2010/02/14/southwest-kevin-smith/

http://mashable.com/2011/12/14/ashton-kutcher-foot-in-mouth-award-tweet/

http://mashable.com/2012/12/12hurricane-sandy-google-search/

http://mattfisher.tumblr.com/post/29338478278/my-sister-paid-progressive-
insurance-to-defend-her

http://mattfisher.tumblr.com/post/29432884849/today-in-response-to-my-blog
-post-entitled-my

http://money.cnn.com/2007/09/17/news/newsmakers/Ken_Chenault.fortune
/index.htm

http://money.cnn.com/2011/09/29/pf/bank_of_america_debit_fee/index.htm

http://money.cnn.com/magazines/fortune/most-admired/2012/snapshots/2068
.html

http://news.van.fedex.com/package-volumes-projected-spike-december-12-fedex
-hits-its-busiest-day-history

http://newsroom.bankofamerica.com/press-release/consumer-banking/bank-america
-will-not-implement-debit-usage-fee

http://pewinternet.org/Reports/2011/Social-Networking-Sites.aspx

http://research.yougov.com

http://socialtimes.com/files/2010/11/FortuneNetflixReedHastings.jpg

http://thehill.com/blogs/on-the-money/banking-financial-institutions/97871-durbin
-wins-battle-to-pass-qinterchange-feeq-legislation

http://thelede.blogs.nytimes.com/2012/10/25/hurricane-sandy-threatens-northeast
-and-mid-atlantic/

http://travel.usatoday.com/flights/post/2011/12/american-issues-statement-on-alec
-baldwin-incident/580193/1

http://twitpic.com/1340gw

http://video.cnbc.com/gallery/?video=3000049613

http://ww5.komen.org/AboutUs/AboutUs.html

http://www.alaskaair.com/content/travel-info/policies/seating-customers-of-size.aspx

http://www.blogsouthwest.com/blog/not-so-silent-bob

http://www.bloomberg.com/news/2011-10-30/-confluence-of-events-led-to-plane
-s-stranding-on-tarmac-jetblue-says.html

http://www.bostonglobe.com/business/2011/12/25/interview-with-bank-america
-ceo-brian-moynihan/8FTV3jGMojNgGqPmqvSKyO/story.html

http://www.burson-marsteller.com/Innovation_and_insights/Thought_Leadership
/Lists/SlideShares/DispForm.aspx?ID=27

http://www.businessinsider.com/heres-the-evidence-that-progressive-is-about-to
-kill-off-flo-2012-8

http://www.businessinsider.com/let-alec-play-zyngas-response-to-baldwins-tussle
-with-american-airlines-2011-12

http://www.cbsnews.com/2100-502303_162-20071227.html

http://www.cbsnews.com/8301-201_162-57489685/komen-founder-to-step-down
-as-chief-executive/

http://www.cbsnews.com/8301-501465_162-57338656-501465/american-airlines
-releases-statement-on-alec-baldwins-accusations/

http://www.cbsnews.com/8301-501465_162-57338656-501465/american-airlines
-releases-statement-on-alec-baldwins-accusations/#postComments

http://www.change.org/petitions/tell-bank-of-america-no-5-debit-card-fees

http://www.charlotteobserver.com/2012/09/02/3497277/banking-anger-in-charlotte
.html

http://www.china.org.cn/china/2011-12/08/content_24101840.htm

http://www.chinadaily.com.cn/bizchina/2013-02/21/content_16243933.htm

http://www.chinadaily.com.cn/china/2011-12/21/content_14300990.htm

http://www.chinahush.com/2011/11/20/china-internet-celebrity-luo-yonghao
-smashes-refrigerators-at-siemens-beijing-headquarters/

http://www.comscore.com/Insights/Presentations_and_Whitepapers/2011/it_is
_a_social_world_top_10_need-to-knows_about_social_networking

http://www.dominosbiz.com/Biz-Public-EN/Extras/Cares/ and http://youtu.be/
dem6eA7-A2I

http://www.dominosbiz.com/Biz-Public-EN/Site+Content/Secondary/About
+Dominos/Fun+Facts/

http://www.eeo.com.cn/ens/2011/1124/216405.shtml

http://www.facebook.com/LetsGetNYCBackonHerFeet?ref=ts&fref=ts

http://www.facebook.com/Nov.Fifth

http://www.fedex.com/in/enews/2013/february/fortune.html

http://www.forbes.com/sites/erikamorphy/2011/12/11/companies-cant-win-the
-twitter-wars-especially-against-the-likes-of-alec-baldwin/

http://www.hcdi.net

http://www.holmesreport.com/featurestories-info/12971/The-Top-12-Crises-Of
-2012-Part-2.aspx

http://www.huffingtonpost.com/2011/09/30/bank-of-america-debit-card-fees_n
_989397.html

http://www.huffingtonpost.com/2012/01/31/komen-for-the-cure-halts-_n_1245320
.html

http://www.huffingtonpost.com/2012/03/28/spike-lee-zimmerman-address-tra
yvon-martin_n_1385071.html

http://www.huffingtonpost.com/adam-hanft/apple-foxconn-china_b_1392339
.html

http://www.huffingtonpost.com/alec-baldwin/american-airlines-service-_b_1135201
.html

http://www.indeed.com/q-Social-Media-jobs.html

http://www.investopedia.com/#axzz2Np8QUcR1

http://www.isnare.com/?aid=616947&ca=Computers+and+Technology.

http://www.jetblue.com/flying-on-jetblue/customer-protection/

http://www.kndo.com/story/15907998/jetblue-passengers-stuck-on-plane-for-7
-hours

http://www.msopr.com/press-releases/uh-huh-her-camila-grey-and-leisha-hailey
-respond-to-southwest-airlines-incident/

http://www.msopr.com/press-releases/uh-huh-her-camila-grey-and-leisha-hailey
-respond-to-southwest-airlines-incident/

http://www.nbc.com/saturday-night-live/video/netflix-apology/1359563/

http://www.nbc.com/saturday-night-live/video/weekend-update-capt-steve-rogers/
1372901/

http://www.newschinamag.com/magazine/top-blogger-profile-luo-yonghao/

http://www.nyrr.org/newsroom/nyrr-news-service/2012-ing-new-york-city
-marathon-cancelled

http://www.nytimes.com/2009/04/16/business/media/16dominos.html

http://www.nytimes.com/2011/06/07/nyregion/timeline-of-weiner-case.html

http://www.nytimes.com/2012/01/26/business/ieconomy-apples-ipad-and-the
-human-costs-for- workers-in-china.html?pagewanted=all

http://www.nytimes.com/2012/02/04/health/policy/komen-breast-cancer-group
-reverses-decision-that-cut-off-planned-parenthood.html?pagewanted=all

http://www.nytimes.com/2012/02/04/health/policy/komen-breast-cancer-group
-reverses-decision-that-cut-off-planned-parenthood.html?pagewanted=all

http://www.nytimes.com/2012/08/18/your-money/progressives-side-of-the-insurance
-case-that-blew-up-on-the-internet.html?pagewanted=all

http://www.nytimes.com/2012/11/03/sports/backlash-builds-as-new-york-city
-marathon-divides-city.html?pagewanted=all

http://www.nytimes.com/2012/11/09/giving/komen-foundation-works-to-regain
-support-after-planned-parenthood-controversy.html?pagewanted=all

http://www.progressive.com/progressive-insurance/core-values.aspx

http://www.progressive.com/understanding-insurance/entries/2012/08/Default.aspx

http://www.progressive.com/understanding-insurance/entries/2012/8/14/statement
_on_fisher.aspx

http://www.progressive.com/understanding-insurance/entries/2012/8/14/statement
_on_fisher.aspx

http://www.prweek.com/uk/news/991636/NestlE-faces-Facebook-crisis-Greenpeace
-rainforest-allegations/

http://www.reuters.com/article/2011/09/29/us-bankofamerica-debit-idUSTRE7
8S4GQ20110929

http://www.reuters.com/article/2011/09/29/us-bankofamerica-debit-idUSTRE7
8S4GQ20110929

http://www.siemens.com/about/en/values-vision-strategy/values.htm

http://www.siemens.com/about/en/worldwide.htm

http://www.socialbrite.org/2011/01/11/guide-to-free-social-media-monitoring-tools/

http://www.southwest.com/html/customer-service/extra-seat/index-pol.html

http://www.southwest.com/html/southwest-difference/community-involvement/
glbt/index.html

http://www.swamedia.com/releases/9063e4d3-dabc-4ab2-9016-fa4c19895894

http://www.swamedia.com/releases/9b8360a2-d68a-4012-b511-0a9579b24b7d

http://www.thedailyshow.com/watch/wed-june-8-2011/the-wangover;   http://www
.thedailyshow.com/watch/mon-june-13-2011/the-wangover-part-ii

http://www.tmz.com/about

http://www.transtats.bts.gov

http://www.united.com/web/en-US/content/travel/specialneeds/customersize/
default.aspx

http://www.vanityfair.com/business/2012/02/netflix-201202

http://www.wantchinatimes.com/news-subclass-cnt.aspx?   id=20111206000092
& cid=1103

http://www.washingtonpost.com/blogs/dr-gridlock/post/alec-baldwin-removed-from
-american-airlines-flight/2011/12/07/gIQAiaKYcO_blog.html

http://www.washingtonpost.com/lifestyle/style/nancy-brinker-the-steely-force-in
-the-susan-g-komen-foundation/2012/02/10/gIQAYjCfER_story.html

http://www.washingtonpost.com/politics/rick-perrys-gop-debate-oops/2011/11/
09/gIQAumzo6M_video.html

http://www.weibo.com

http://www.weibo.com/laoluoyonghao

http://www.whitehouse.gov/economy/middle-class/dodd-frank-wall-street-reform

http://www.youtube.com/watch?v=7r4e5Wg4PDI Tiger Woods

http://www.youtube.com/watch?v=bAW2LPRn0vQ

http://www.youtube.com/watch?v=Hiz5EtNxtc8

http://www.youtube.com/watch?v=j4XT-l-_3y0

http://www.youtube.com/watch?v=L0z5k0mc5yk

http://www.youtube.com/watch?v=lgj6NEk9xEw

http://www.youtube.com/watch?v=PKUDTPbDhnA

http://www.youtube.com/watch?v=PKUDTPbDhnA for FedEx and http://youtu.be/1D9PikBzNNo for Domino's Pizza.

http://www.youtube.com/watch?v=Xs8nseNP4s0 Exxon.

http://www.youtube.com/watch?v=Y5UoTWAMQwU

http://www.youtube.com/watch?v=Zb2vkbK66RY

http://www1.cnnic.cn/IDR/ReportDownloads/201209/t20120928_36586.htm

http://wwwmediabistro.com/alltwitter/twitter-active-total-users_b17655

http://youtu.be/1D9PikBzNNo

http://youtu.be/4ESU_PcqI38

http://youtu.be/c8Tn8n5CIPk

http://youtu.be/itDejkU20Ig

http://youtu.be/qvLDFtaL5HI

http://youtu.be/-r_PIg7EAUw

http://youtu.be/rRFwcN_EOSU

https://twitter.com/BarackObama

https://twitter.com/Qwikster

https://twitter.com/search?q=%23letalecplay&src=typd

https://twitter.com/ThatKevinSmith

https://www.facebook.com/groups/295542063792908/?ref=ts&fref=ts

https://www.facebook.com/ingnycm?ref=ts&fref=ts

ING New York City Marathon, *Facebook* (2012)

Kubler-Ross, E. (2004). *Celestial arts: On life after death*. Berkeley, CA.

McGoldrick, H., *Runner's World*. (2012, November 2) (http://www.runnersworld.com/) (http://www.runnersworld.com/races/nyc-marathon-re-branded-race-recover-0)

Michael, D., & Zhou, S. (2010, August 2). *How to Sell Online in China* Bloomberg Businessweek (http://www.businessweek.com/globalbiz/content/aug2010/gb2010082_947892.htm)

New York Road Runners, *Website* (2012).

Orwell, G. (1950). *1984* New York, Penguin Group (USA) Incorporated.

Qualman, E. (2012). *Socialnomics*. New York: John Wiley & Sons.

Scott, D. (2010). *The New Rules of Marketing + PR* (Incorporated page 47). Hoboken, NJ: John Wiley & Sons.

Stacks, Don W. Lecture material on crisis communication and management. University of Miami School of Communication, Coral Gables, FL.

Wall Street Journal. (2012), www.online.wsj.com

Xinhuanet. (2010) (http://news.xinhuanet.com/english2010/2010-01/18/c _13140680.htm)

Index

A
Action plans, 120
Airline crisis, 73–75

B
Bank of America
  background details, 47–48
  crisis
    bank's response, 50–51
    further fallout, 51
    lessons learned, 51–52
    public responses, 49–50
    resolution, 51
  parting thoughts, 53–54
Business decisions, 117–118

C
China Internet Network Information
    Center (CNNIC), 98
China, social media, 98–99
Chinese Internet culture, 98
CNNIC. *See* China Internet Network
    Information Center
Communication plans, 120
Credibility, 16
Crisis
  American *vs.* Alec Baldwin, 69–73
  Bank of America, 49–52
  categories, 9
  chances in, 9–10
  definition, 8–9
  Domino's Pizza, 111–115
  FedEx, 108–110
  JetBlue, 56–58
  Komen, Susan G., 18, 22
  preparedness, 120
  principles for professionals, 13–14
  Progressive insurance, 87–96
  recovery, 16
  Siemens, 97–105
  and social media, 11–13
  Southwest Airlines, 59–69
Crisis leaders, 15

D
Diffused publics, 122
Domino's Pizza
  background details, 111
  company's response, 112–113
  crisis, 111–112
  lessons learned, 114–115

E
Enabling publics, 122

F
FedEx
  background details, 108
  company's response, 109–110
  crisis, 108–109
  lessons learned, 110
Functional publics, 122

H
Human behavior, 9

J
JetBlue
  background details, 56–57
  chain of mistakes, 58
  crisis, 57–58
  lessons learned, 58

K
Komen, Susan G.
  background details, 17–18
  crisis, 18, 22
  key mistakes, 19–21
  learning from mistakes, 21–22
  parting thoughts, 22–23
Kutcher, Ashton, 41–45

L
Lee-Bernoff model, 6

M
Management failures, 9

N

Natural disasters, 9
Netizen, 98
New York City (NYC) Marathon
    communication, 83–84
    crisis debate, 80–81
    fallout, 82–83
    lessons learned, 84
    parting thoughts, 84–85
    retracing, 81–82
New York Road Runners (NYRR),
    79–80
Normative publics, 122
NYRR. *See* New York Road Runners

O

Online social media, 98

P

Planned Parenthood, 18–19
Progressive insurance
    background details, 87–88
    chain of mistakes, 92–94
    crisis, 89–92
    lessons learned, 95
    parting thoughts, 95–96
Public relation professionals, 7–8
Publics, 122

S

Selective empathy, 105
Self-inflected crises, 39
Self-inflicted harm, 118–119
Siemens
    background details, 97–99
    crisis, 99–102
    lessons learned, 102–104
    parting thoughts, 104–105
Social media
    characteristics, 5–6

    in China, 98–99
    communication, 15
    conversation, 15
    and crisis, 11–13
    crisis factors, 2
    definition, 6
    influencing factors, 120–123
    landscape, 3–4
    online, 98
    and planning, 120
    and public relations, 4–7
    public relations professionals,
        7–8
    responsibilities, 7
Social media experts, 7–8
Social networking sites, 3–4
Southwest Airlines
    background details, 59
    first crisis
        chain of mistakes, 63–64
        description, 59–61
        lessons learned, 64–65
        responses, 61–63
    second crisis
        chain of mistakes, 68
        description, 66–67
        lessons learned, 69
        responses, 67–68
    Spectators, 6

T

Twitter
    Kutcher, Ashton, 41–45
    parting thoughts, 45–46
    self-inflected crises, 39
    social media crisis, 37–39
    Weiner, Anthony, 39–41

W

Weiner, Anthony, 39–41

Announcing the Business Expert Press Digital Library

Concise E-books Business Students Need for Classroom
and Research

This book can also be purchased in an e-book collection by your library as
- a one-time purchase,
- that is owned forever,
- allows for simultaneous readers,
- has no restrictions on printing, and
- can be downloaded as PDFs from within the library community.

Our digital library collections are a great solution to beat the rising cost of textbooks. e-books can be loaded into their course management systems or onto student's e-book readers.

The **Business Expert Press** digital libraries are very affordable, with no obligation to buy in future years. For more information, please visit **www.businessexpertpress.com/librarians**. To set up a trial in the United States, please contact **Adam Chesler** at *adam.chesler@ businessexpertpress.com* for all other regions, contact **Nicole Lee** at *nicole.lee@igroupnet.com*.